A History of Drums Made in Germany
And the Companies Behind Them

By Fritz Steger

Anthology, Layout and Editing by Horst Büttgen (†)
Additional Editing by Martin Heidinger and Guido Schmidt

Translation Gina Billy

I would like to begin by offering a very special thank you to Ingo Winterberg. His invaluable assistance and wealth of subject-specific knowledge greatly contributed to moving the crucial phases of this project forwards.

My heartfelt thanks also goes to:
Hansjörg Reichenbach, Mike Bufton and Christine Marques for their support. To Rob Cook, who´s e-mail came just at the right time. And to Harald Wieland (†), who graciously shared his amazing contacts and stories from 40 years in the music business.

Portions of this book appeared in "Drums & Percussion" magazine, and I would like to say a special thanks to Heinz Kronberger for his support of this project.

Additionally, I am extremely grateful to all of those who supported this project with material or information.

Fritz Steger, Rehlingstraße 12a, 79100 Freiburg / Germany
steger@drumhouse.com

Rebeats Edition 2023

ISBN: 978-1-888408-63-8

Copyright ©2023

All rights reserved. No part of this publication may be reproduced, stored in a retrieval system, or transmitted in any form or by any means, electronic, mechanical, photocopying, recording or otherwise, without the prior written permission of the copyright holder.

	Capital	*Page*
1.	Foreword	3
2.	Introduction	5
3.	Construction of drums before WW II	7
4.	Sonor since 1875	13
5.	Trixon 1947-> ~1973	29
6.	Deri 1946->1960	41
7.	Rimmel 1960 -> ~1990	47
8.	Specials	57
9.	Tromsa 1946 -> ~1990	75
10.	Lefima since 1861	81
11.	Offelder 1955 - 1975	89
12.	Korri, Lindberg and others	95
13.	Construction of drums in the GDR	103
14.	Sources	109
15.	Alphabetical Index	110
16.	Further information	112

The History of Drums Made In Germany

Around the year 2005

I found myself in the old part of the city of Marburg eating dinner alone at an Indian restaurant. During my meal, I started thinking about why there are many books about American manufacturers with German origins, such as Ludwig or Gretsch, etc., but that German manufacturers are in danger of sinking completely into oblivion. So I took a paper napkin and sketched the outline for this book and started researching. My quest for information ended up taking me all over Germany making interviews with the descendants of company founders, former employees, and collectors. When available, I was able to make use of information from company archives and the German patent office.

In the following year, Heinz Kronberger gave me the opportunity of creating a series about German manufacturers for Germanys Drums & Percussion magazine. The idea of a book was still following me around, but it didn't really get off the ground until I hooked up with the author of the book "Trix on Trixon", Ingo Winterberg, who agreed to take over the book's coordination and layout.

But it would still be a long way to go. It turned out to be much more difficult than expected to find a suitable publisher. Time passed, changes were made and then rejected. In 2019 I wrote to Rob Cook the author of various books on the history of drums asking if he saw an opportunity to publish my book. I didn't hear from him back and in the spring of 2023, I decided to finally bury this project. At exactly that moment and at the right time, Rob's answer came, and now you are holding the final result in your hands.

Nevertheless, the puzzle is far from being finished and I am a long way from being able to claim that every detail is complete or correct. Here as well, I can only provide a general profile of the numerous German manufacturers. My hope is that as many drum enthusiasts all over the world keep drums made in Germany and companies behind them in their heart and mind.

Fritz Steger October 2023

Drums Made in Germany

At first glance, a book called "Drums Made in Germany" could make you expect to see something along the lines - and length – of a first grade reader. After all, if you make a list of the few German drum and drum set manufacturing companies, it will be quite short and might lead you to conclude that there really isn't much say about this topic ... or is there?

If you think back though, images such as oval-shaped bass drums or ones with flattened contours or even made in rectangular forms start coming up from the recesses of your mind.
Although the list of names is not long, there are very famous ones on it. The makers of these brands had an innate, limitless sense of idealism and at times, an incredible adventurous spirit that are reflected in the innovations they brought to the world of drum making. Just remember: Rimmel and his oval bass drum and one of the first manufacturers of synthetic heads;
Lefima and the first parallel snare strainer or SONOR and the first double pedal in 1927.
Just "Google" for ten minutes and you will quickly get hits for entire fan communities, like the one on the Trixon website.

Drum manufactures with names like "Korri" or "Derri" that have now almost been completely forgotten also had their places in history – and this long before the drum set appeared on the scene.
The vagaries of World War II and its aftermath meant that most German instrument manufactures shared a similar fate. Many of them lost almost everything they had during this time, and most of them had to start over from almost scratch. The War brought hard times to all. Even though new names did appear on the scene then, most of them did not last long and their businesses disappeared at the latest with the fall of the Berlin wall.

It is wonderful that, although few in number, there are German drum manufactures with the quality seal "Made in Germany" who have remained competitive on the international market.
And then Fritz Steger comes along and buckles down to the task of digging up and breathing life into long forgotten names and stories, shedding new light on the history of German manufactures and reminding us all of details in danger of being lost forever.
"Drums Made in Germany" works totally and it successfully provides an interesting collection of facts and information from way back when that had almost sunk into oblivion.

Karl-Heinz Menzel
Managing Director
SONOR GmbH
2000 – 2017

The History of Drums Made In Germany

CONSTRUCTION OF DRUMS BEFORE WW II

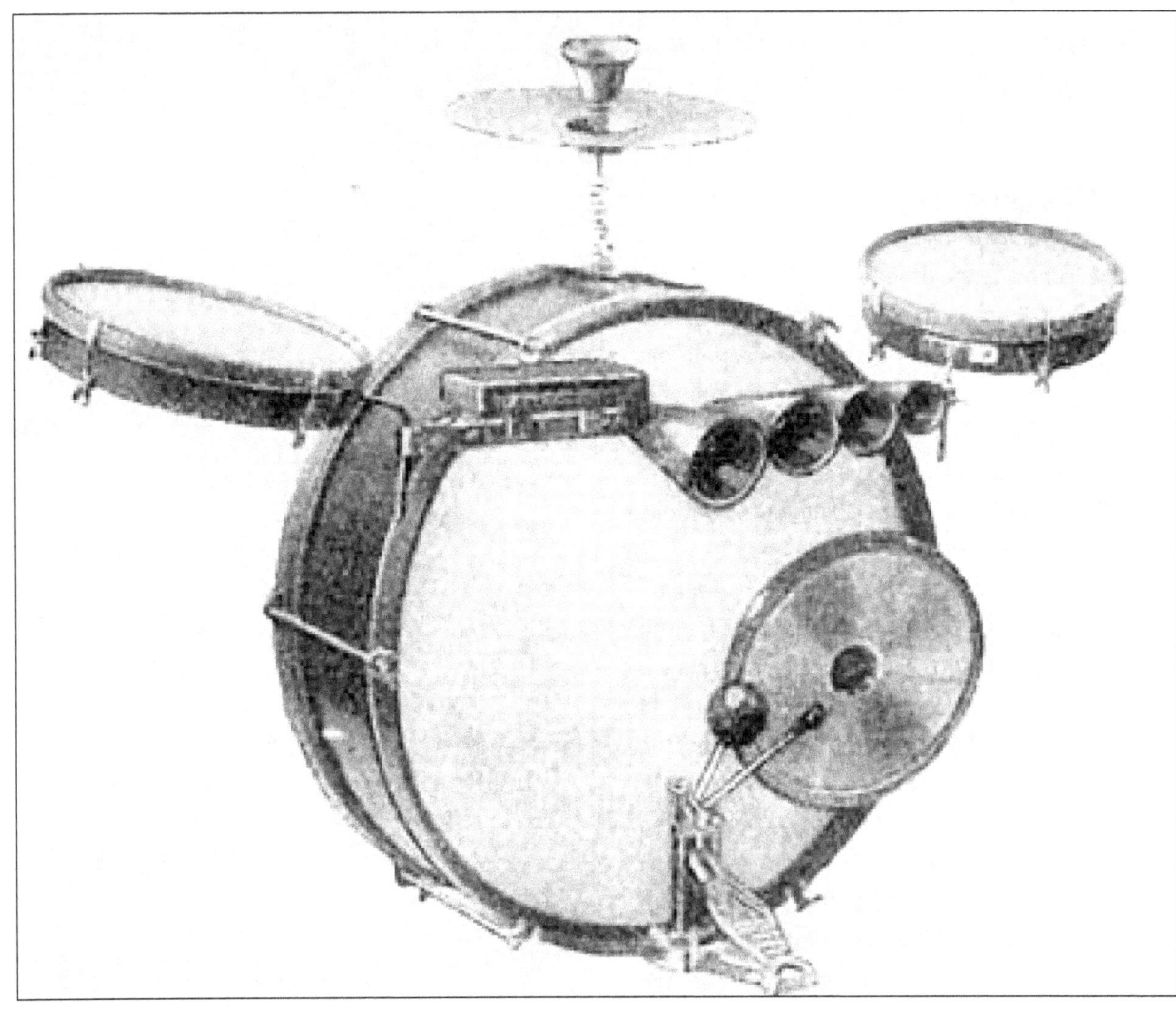

The History of Drums Made In Germany

The history of American drum manufacturers has been well-documented in numerous publications. To date, though, almost no one has shown much interest in the German manufacturers. However, the history of drum manufacture in America is also partly German, as Theobald and William Ludwig or Friedrich Gretsch, for example, were all German immigrants who brought the art of German drum manufacturing with them to their new homeland. A huge problem arises when trying to tell the story of the German manufacturers because so many drawings and catalogues were destroyed during the two world wars.

For this reason, even tradition-rich companies like Sonor have gaps in their archives. During the research about the manufacturers, it was still possible to speak with first-hand witnesses about the years following World War II. But the years prior to it remain partially a puzzle that, unfortunately, has many important missing pieces.

The history of drums is also the history of human beings. A false assumption often connects the drum exclusively with Africa, but there is hardly any culture in which the drum has not played some sort of role. Over the ages, percussion instruments have been, among other things, a means of communication, cult objects, used to set the pace for marching and in various forms of therapy.

The snare drum originated in the military and can be traced back to the tambour in the Middle Ages that was normally played to accompany a flute.

Around the middle of the 19th century, the snare drum was increasingly included in symphony orchestras. It was most often made of metal that was bent into form by brass instrument makers. That's why up until the not so distant past, those practicing this trade were also allowed to use the professional designation of "drum maker".

Catalog shot mid 1920s

CONSTRUCTION OF DRUMS BEFORE WW II

The bass drum arrived in Europe by way of Turkish Janissary music. These bass drums were – and still are – constructed of wood, and in rural areas were often made by carpenters or coopers.

Cymbals got their start in Asia and also came to Central Europe through Janissary music. They were incorporated first into military, and then later into symphony orchestras. Cymbals play an important role in military music as they are used with the bass drum to set the beat.

The drum set, which is the subject of this book, appeared relatively late in the history of drums in the middle of the 19th century.

Numerous publications credit New Orleans as being the birth place of the drum set.

This, however, is not really correct. The truth is that experiments with various apparatuses that allowed one person to play on several drums at the same time were being conducted on various continents simultaneously.

Lefima »Low Boy« Charleston machine

At this time, German catalogs depicted a device with a pedal used to operate a bass drum and cymbals. The snare drum, though, was at a sort of stand-still and played whilst seated. It was later joined by the "Low Boy", a predecessor of the Hi-hat.

Further developments led to additional percussion instruments being attached to the bass drum, and then later, to a movable console.

The tom-tom, which originated in China, was used to supplement the drums and appeared more and more often.

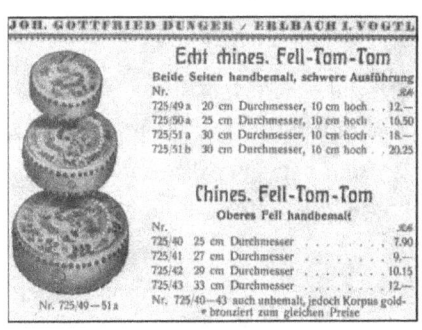

Catalogue shots 1920s

9

The History of Drums Made In Germany

The pre-war drum manufacturers that remain well-known today are:
Lefima in Markneukirchen (founded in 1861, it is the oldest of known drum manufactures); **Sonor** in Weißenfels/Saale (founded in 1875); the Dresdner Trommel-und Apparatebau - **Spenke & Metz, GPL** (Gustav Pouchard Leipzig) and **Walter Pelzner** (Hannover). Most likely, though, every larger city had workshops where drums and/or other instruments were made.

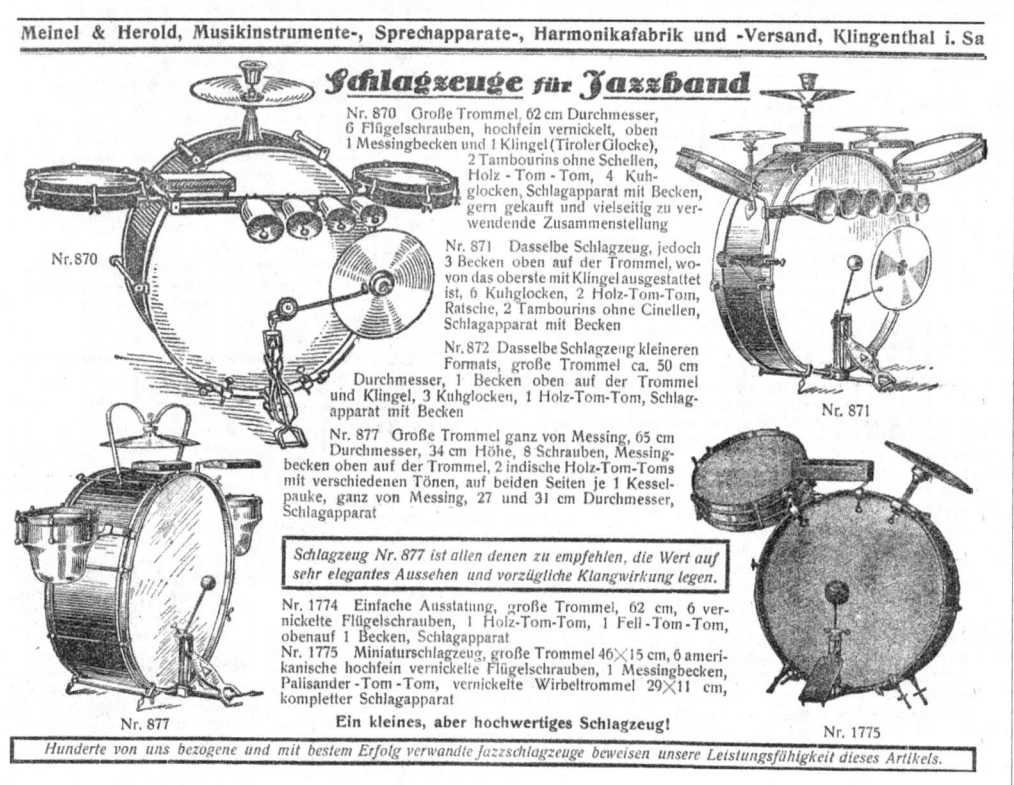

Catalogue shot 1920s

As already mentioned, the making of drums in rural areas was carried out by practitioners of other trades and many examples of their instruments can still be found today. Unfortunately, these do not bear any type of trade mark which makes it impossible to assign them to a particular manufacturer.
Many of these workshops only produced the shell and used the services of specialty suppliers for mechanics and hardware.

Quite a few of these suppliers had settled in Germany's so-called "Musikwinkel" [music triangle] (Markneukirchen/ Klingenthal) in the Saxon Vogtland. The separation between instrument manufacturing and distribution got an early start here and by the middle of the 19th century, was quite wide-spread.

CONSTRUCTION OF DRUMS BEFORE WW II

Specialization and manufacturers increasingly using division of labor were typical in this region. At that time, the music city of Markneukirchen had 61 wholesalers and 35 retailers. These businesses purchased goods by the dozen from independent instrument makers and then sent them on throughout the German Empire. The wholesalers who shipped the instruments were called "Fortschicker" (which translates loosely as "consigner") and they brought prosperity to the region. By 1945, up to 21 millionaires were said to be living in the region.

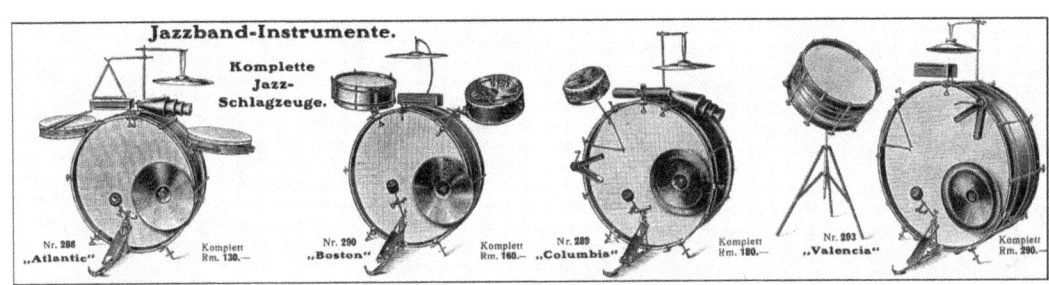

The Schuster Brothers (Markneukirchen) Catalogue shot late 1920s

Catalogue shot early 1920s

Catalogue shot late 1930s

Markneukirchen was temporarily home to the second largest number of taxpayers (per head) in Saxon. Famous consignors from those days were: Adler; Kruse; Scherzer; Schuster & Co. in Markneukirchen; Gewa (Georg Walter, today the importer of, i.e., DW, Remo, Gibraltar, Gretsch, LP, Toca and Paiste) in Adorf; Wunderlich in Siebenbrunn; Dunger in Erlbach; Meinel & Herold and Hess in Klingenthal (Saxon).

In all likelihood, it will no longer be possible to discover the manufacturers of all the producers of superb German drums.

The History of Drums Made In Germany

The History of Drums Made In Germany

Percussion instruments
Drum factory
Johs. Link KG
Aue/Westfalen
Since 1875

When one thinks about German drum manufacturers, the first name that comes to mind is **Sonor**. This company can look back at over 135 years of tradition and is still going strong today.

Its founder **Johannes Link** was a trained wood turner and tanner who was born in 1847 in Nördlingen in Bavaria. In 1875, he opened a small workshop in Weißenfels on the river Saale and began producing drumheads and simple military drums. Although he started off humbly with only one employee, business soon began to boom. In 1878, he expanded the production site and relocated to the Leipziger Street. The production palate kept increasing and around 1900, it included the manufacture of timpani, concert drums, xylophones, cymbals, triangles and smaller percussion instruments. By then, 53 employees were working for Johannes Link. In 1907, the name "Sonor," which has Latin roots and means "the sound," was registered with the Imperial Patent Office. The catalog from the same year depicted an apparatus that combined a bass drum and cymbals that was the predecessor of pedals and Hi-hats.

Johannes Link 1847 – 1914

Ad circa 1900

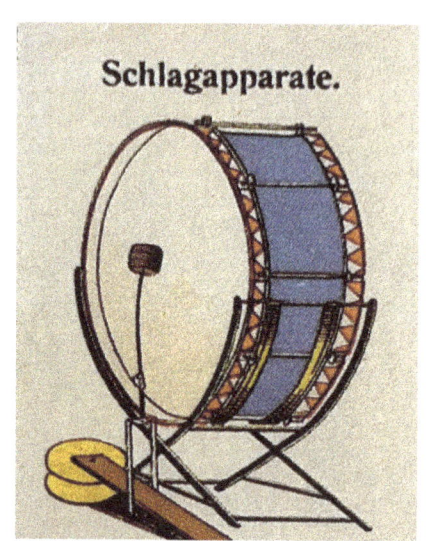

Catalogue shot 1907

Johannes Link died in 1914 and his son **Otto Link** guided the business through the turmoil of WW I and the following years of depression. A second factory was opened in 1917. When most of the Leipziger Street site was destroyed by a fire in 1919, a nearby factory called "Am Bad" was acquired. In addition to his work as head of the company, Otto Link was increasingly involved in international relations with Sweden and was named Consul to Sweden.

Around 1925, Sonor employed 145 workers and was one of the largest businesses of its kind. The plant in Weißenfels was completely modernized in this year and further production sites were opened in order to keep up with the rising demand for Sonor instruments.

This was also when the first real Sonor drum catalog was issued.

Konsul Otto Link 1884 - 1955

Price list cover 1899

Sonor factory in Weißenfels 1919

50th anniversary ceremony 1925

The History of Drums Made In Germany

In the first half of its history, the company can be credited with many innovations. These include: the world's first pedal machine; a parade drum with wooden hoops; presumably the first double-pedal - used for striking bass drum and cymbals simultaneously; and a drum that could be tuned with knobs.

At this time, jazz was also becoming more well-known in Europe and special instruments were developed and built for this musical style. The first special catalog devoted to jazz instruments appeared in 1930. Otto Link strived to keep the company on course during the Great Depression, WW II and the post-war years.

1936

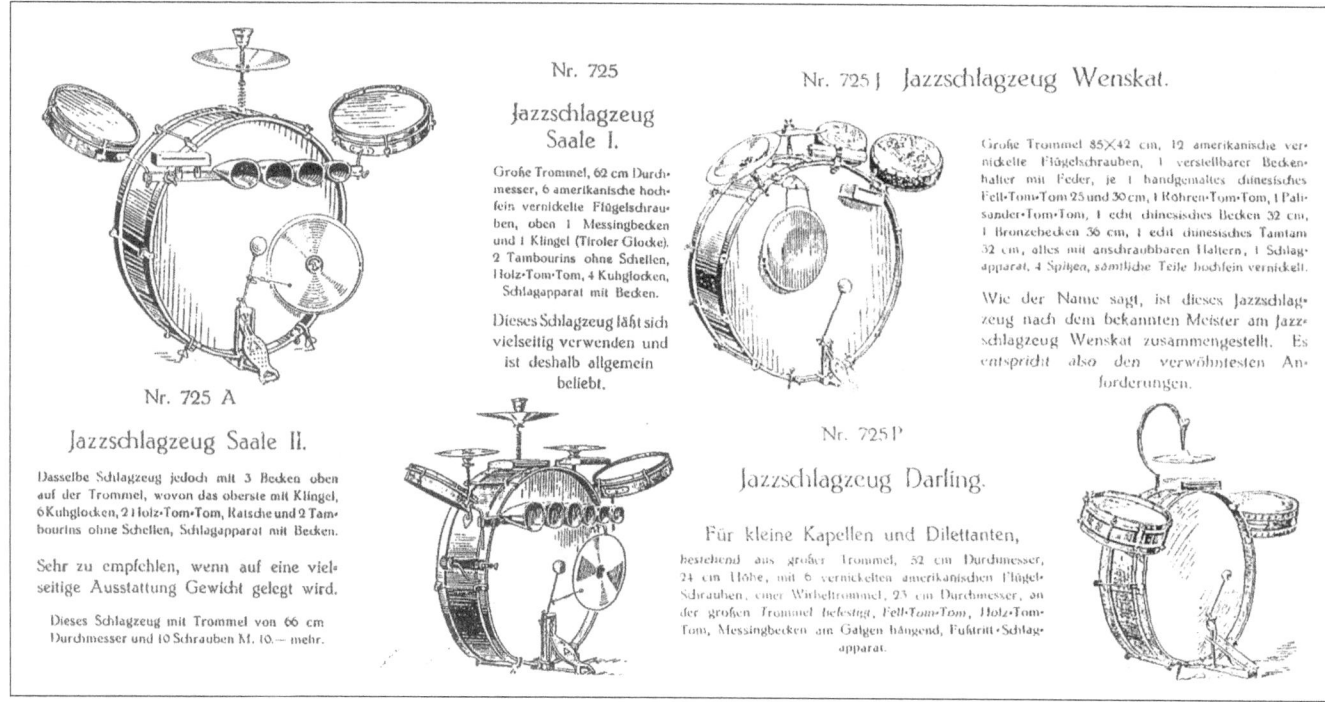

Catalogue shots 1930

Following the division of Germany, the order was given to expropriate the company and arrest its owner. The Russian occupation forces seized and nationalized Sonor, and from then on, its production facilities were called TROWA VEB Instruments. Otto Link just managed to escape imminent arrest by risking a daring escape with his son Horst Link to West Berlin. According to an article in "Music Trades Magazine," Horst Link used a rented ambulance and forged papers to bring his father across the German-German border. From Berlin, they flew to West Germany and once there, the family decided to start over from scratch. In 1950, they founded a new Sonor production facility in Aue in Westphalia.

SONOR

The black and white catalog from 1952 already included the entire product palette from marching drums to combined sets with contemporary names of the day such as "Luxus" and "Super".

Sonor »Luxus« 1952

Sonor »Super« 1952

The palette was expanded in 1953 with the Orff instruments and these remain an important pillar in the company today. Additionally, the fact that Sonor could draw on its 50 years of drum building experience gave it a head start against other postwar manufacturers such as Deri or Tromsa.

Ad in "Jazz-Podium" magazine 1955

The History of Drums Made In Germany

At first, production continued in the manner used in the 1940s, but Sonor drums quickly surpassed the competition in both design and quality. Only the company Trixon with its innovative ideas and modern image could really challenge Sonor's market position.

Otto Link died in 1955 and his son Horst Link took over at Sonor's helm. He continually expanded production and the production palette. In 1956, the Sonor musical instrument catalog featured over 100 pages.

The sets in this black and white catalog bore English names such as "Star" or "King". Several famous jazz musicians of the day, such as Kenny Clarke, played Sonor instruments.
Catalogue shots 1956

Another important factor that contributed to Sonor's success was its takeover (at first jointly with competitor Trixon) of the American cymbal manufacturer Zildjian in the early 1960s. This is also when the catalog in color showed for the first time the classic Sonor mallet logo as well as the slim teardrop lugs - the synonym for design and fine quality "Made in Germany". However, the drum sets carried the names of American cities such as "Chicago" or "Memphis" and Latin American instruments such as bongos and congas were also included in the range.

SONOR

In the mid 1960s, the heyday for Ludwig began when a certain Ringo Starr made sure that in faraway Chicago, all eyes were on him and his hip Ludwig set. Young Sonor drum players were relegated to the sidelines of the "un-cool" dance musicians, while Ludwig had to implement triple-shifts just to keep up with demand.

Despite this, Horst Link presented Sonor in 1966 on page 2 of the catalog as being a traditional, German family business. Page 2 of the catalog included pictures of himself, his first wife Helga and the children Jörg (depicted on the drums in the catalog) Andreas (on the double bass) and Angelika (on metallophone).

Sonor "Chicago" catalogue 1963

The History of Drums Made In Germany

At the end of the 1960s, drums produced less expensively in Japan arrived in Germany. The music company Roland Meinl in Franconia began importing the brands Star (later Tama) and for a short time, Pearl. Other so-called "stencil brands" that carried catchy names like "Drum Mate" or "Zen-On," effected changes in the drum market. One of Horst Link's most valuable business decisions was that he – as opposed to his American competitors – took this new development seriously and reacted quickly. This was certainly one of the reasons that led to Sonor being one of the world's most successful manufacturers in the 1980s while companies such as Ludwig and Gretsch found themselves struggling. Some firms, like Rogers and Slingerland, even had to close down.

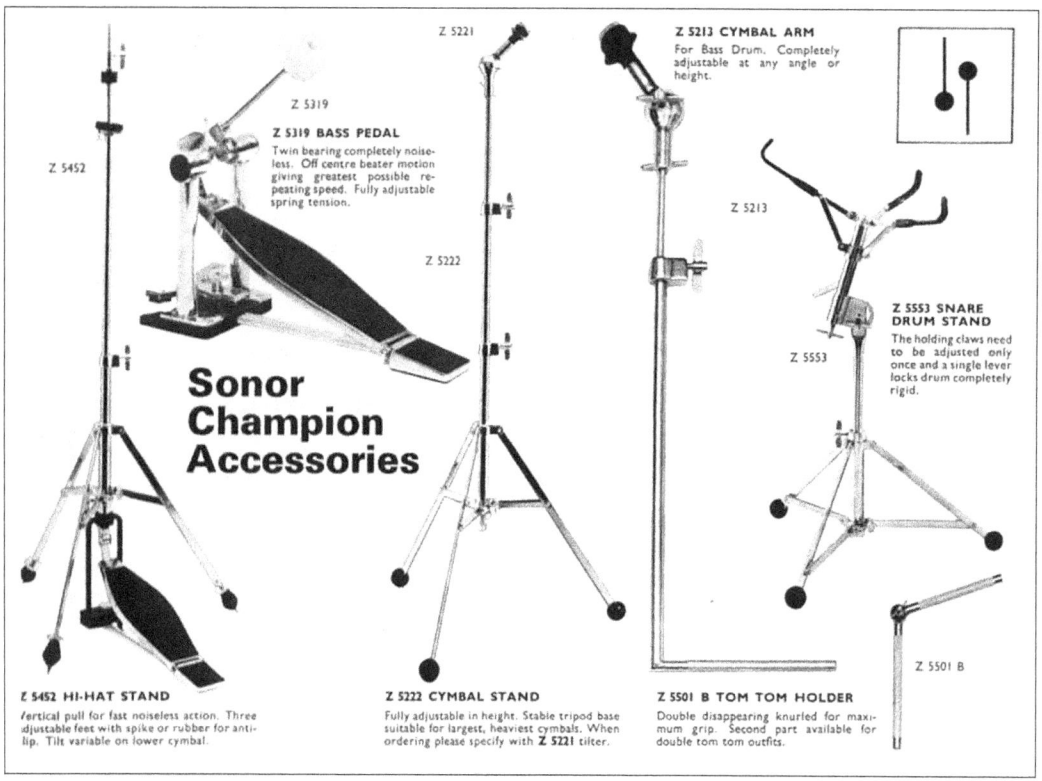

Sonor catalogue 1971

As opposed to the Japanese, Sonor introduced lighter hardware with varying price categories in the "Standard" and "Champion" lines, but did not modify the shells.

These changes didn't affect sound quality, though, and it remained better than the Japanese competition. The machine-pressed Tyrko cymbals also helped reduce costs. In the top-range, new, square lugs replaced the Teardrop – similar to the way box bumpers appeared on the VW Beetle.

SONOR

In 1971, Sonor used its less-expensive, "Swinger" series with square lugs to become one of the first manufacturers in the world to divide its products into several production lines – a practice that today is practically indispensable. Before this time, there were of course other manufacturers offering stripped-down "student versions," however, a second product line running concurrently was completely new. The drums in this cheaper series used the same beech shell as the more expensive line, however costs were saved by using cheaper hardware and synthetic lugs that were partially produced in the Far East - here a certain similarity to the Ludwig design was hard to overlook.

Sonor »Swinger« catalogue 1972

The "Rocker 2000" series in the colors pink and violet pearl appeared as a budget line in 1973. The "Swinger" received new lugs and was offered as a middle-line product.
From then on, the top series was called "Sonor Champion".

Sonor »K120 Rocker« catalogue 1973

The History of Drums Made In Germany

In 1975, Sonor celebrated its 100 year anniversary with a huge event in Bad Berleburg. Emphasis was once again placed on having a competitive edge through quality and state of the art German engineering. Several very fine hardware features demonstrated that Sonor was set for the future. In this sense, the new "Top of the Champion" line was called "Super Champion".

Sonor »K 103 B The Big Beat – Super Champion« catalogue 1975

A short time later, the "Super Champion" series was re-named to "Phonic" and the "Swinger" series to "Action by Sonor".

»Action by Sonor« catalogue 1976

SONOR

In 1977, Karl Heinz Menzel joined the company and would later play a fateful role in Sonor's fortunes.
At first, he was responsible for creating special models, such as drum sets for product endorsers. With time, though, he influenced more and more the brand's product design.

Karl Heinz Menzel

Oliver Link, the fourth generation of the Link family, greatly influenced company marketing strategy for almost 15 years. He was responsible for "The Drummer's Drum" - one of the most comprehensive catalogs in drum history and one that has been re-worked several times since.

By the end od the 1970's, Horst Link planned a "super drum". It was designed to show clients and competitors everything that "made in Germany" could make possible and was called the "Signature" series.
This is a term that almost every manufacturer uses today in some form or other. But back then, it was used for the first time to designate a magnificent drum.
Its shell had noble surfaces of Bubinga, Makassar or ebony veneer, rectangular shell dimensions and thickly-applied chrome wherever the eye could see. It was built for eternity. Even though it cost the same as a middle class automobile, the series that bore Horst Link's signature was a roaring success.

Catalogue »The Drummer's Drum« 1980/81

Sonor Signature badge

The History of Drums Made In Germany

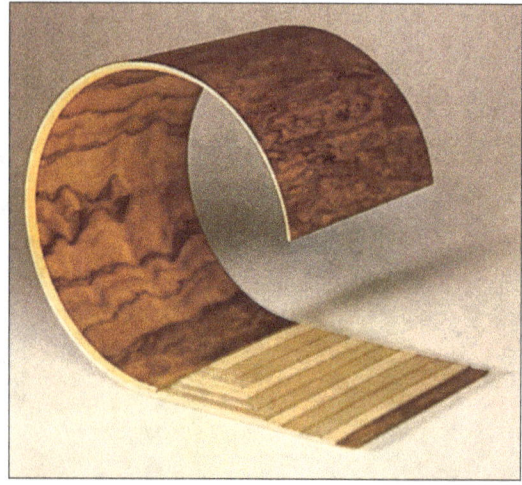

Sonor Signature
Deep, 12-ply wooden shell

Important endorsers such Steve Smith (Journey) and Phil Rudd (AC/DC) did their parts to ensure that Sonor sets now – at the latest – were numbered amongst the best drums in the world and Smith and Rudd have remained loyal to the brand for over 30 years.

Steve Smith (Journey)   *Catalogue 1983*   *Phil Rudd (AC/DC)*

Sonor »Signature« catalogue 1987

Around the same time, Sonor stopped running Zildjian and took over wholesale operations for the company Sabian. Its founder, Bob Zildjian, at that time owned about 5% of Sonor's stock.

In the mid 1980s, the trend once again returned to shorter, and above all, thinner shells. Sonor responded with its successful series "Lite".
Up to this time, Sonor drums had been made of beech wood, but increasing globalization contributed to the "Lite" series being constructed from Scandinavian birch.
At the end of the 1980s, Sonor presented the "Hilite" series made of maple. It and the very successful mid-class series "Force" bore, at the latest, clear signs of Karl Heinz Menzel's work.

Sonor Lite catalogue 1983

The series for beginners called "International" was now being made completely in Taiwan. At the end of the decade, the meanwhile 70-year Horst Link, had to face the fact that none of his children wanted to take over the family business as they were all pursuing other careers. He therefore decided to sell the company to Hohner-AG in Trossingen. A rocky period for Sonor began after the sale. Hohner was already battling various difficulties and had attempted with the purchase of Sonor to obtain a certain image. Hohner employees took over parts of the Sonor management and Karl Heinz Menzel left the company due to differences of opinion and started his own music business. In 1993, the "Designer" series designed by Menzel appeared on the market.

Sonor Designer Drumset 1994

Models built under the new management such as the "S-Class" and "Sonic" series that had unconventional design elements and incorporated synthetic materials in some of the hardware, were not popular with customers. Even long-term employees were unsatisfied with product quality at this time.

The History of Drums Made In Germany

The company Hohner/Sonor was facing more and more difficulties and these eventually led to shares being sold to an investor group from the Far East. Step by step, Sonor was led back to being independent and the management expert Stefan Althoff was put in charge of running the company.

Stefan Althoff

Sonor Sonic-Plus II and S-Class 1995

In 1997, Karl-Heinz Menzel once again took over product development.
The problematic series were either immediately adapted to comply with general tastes or in time, completely replaced.
Menzel and Althoff have been managing the company jointly since 2000.

Globalization meant that that it was soon no longer possible to produce the beginner and mid-class series in Germany. This led to the - at that time - bold decision to transfer production of the newly re-introduced "Force" series to Tianjin, China.

This turned out to be a wise choice because the "Force" series has established itself as a big player on the global market.

Sonor celebrated its 125th anniversary in 2000 in Bad Berleburg and an unforgettable highlight was the performance of the long-time Sonor endorser Bernhard Purdie.

The "Delight" series also made its appearance and filled the gap between the "S-Class" and the "Designer" series. The "Force" series is expanded and re-worked every odd year, i.e. 2001, 2003...etc.

Sonor Force 3000 1994

SONOR

Horst Link 1921 - 2004

On February 2, 2004, Horst Link, the man who was responsible for Sonor's rise to the very top amongst the world's drum makers, died at the age of 85 in Vienna.

In 2007, the "SQ²" was introduced. This new drum system uses the possibility of combining drums virtually via internet to help simplify processes for production and clients. Customers can use a configurator online to put together their dream set from an almost endless number of options.

In 2010 Sonor reintroduced beechwood shells to the market with the the mid-range Ascent series made in China and the limited high end series Beech Infinite series made in Germany. 2012 the Prolite Series (maple) was introduced. Followed up by the Special Edition Birch Infinite 2013 and the Vintage series (beech) in 2015.

Karl-Heinz Menzel took over responsibility for North American business in 2017. He retired in 2020 after 44 years of service to Sonor. From then on, Stefan Althoff was the sole managing director.

In 2017 the SQ1 series (birch) was introduced and from 2018 onwards, the Force series was rebranded as AQ1, AQ2 and AQ-X series.

Since 2020 Arthur Chuang is the new managing director of Matthias Hohner GmbH, Hohner Musikinstrumente GmbH and Sonor GmbH. He took over the tasks from long-time managing director Stefan Althoff, who left Hohner for personal reasons.

Despite the completely new situation in the drum market, Sonor is, at the time of this writing, the last remaining large drum manufacturer that has managed to maintain and continuously expand its drum production in Europe.

Sonor Fabrik in Aue/Bad Berleburg in Nordrhein-Westfalen 2009

1907   1952   1961   1975   1989   1991

The History of Drums Made In Germany

TRIXON

Trixon

1947 – 1973

The History of Drums Made In Germany

Musikinstrumenten-Fabrik Karl-Heinz Weimer KG
1947 – 1973

The second German drum manufacturer to be described here enjoys enormous popularity today in vintage circles throughout the world.

This is, of course, the company Trixon. During the 1950s and 1960s, Trixon gained a significant share of the German market and at that time, enjoyed more international acclaim than almost any other German manufacturer.

The company's founder was Karl-Heinz Weimer, who was born into a musically-inclined family on April 2, 1917. In the 1930s, he studied timpani in Stuttgart and played gigs in local cafés with his brother and sister. During WW II, he served as a drummer with a cavalry regiment.

After the war ended, Weimer quickly recognized the need for percussion instruments, especially amongst musicians in the American and British armies. After receiving permission from the British occupation, he opened a small, one-man workshop at Flüggestraße 1 in the Winterhude section of Hamburg on September 18, 1947. He quickly outgrew the premises there and relocated to Habichtstraße 72 in Hamburg-Barmbek where he began a type of serial production. Karl-Heinz Weimer soon found investors for his growing enterprise and on October 10, 1952, Trixon became a limited partnership. At the beginning of the 1950s, Trixon was already firmly established in the market and in addition to drum sets, also carried many other percussion instruments like congas, bongos and timbales. His passion for the vibraphone led Karl-Heinz Weimer to include from the very start various models of this instrument in his program. The legendary vibraphone player Lionel Hampton got them effectively noticed in the music scene.

Karl-Heinz Weimer with Bob Zildjian in the early 1950s

Lionel Hampton in the early 1950s

30

TRIXON

Customer service was one of Weimer's top priorities and so he introduced the brochure for lessons called "Trix on Trixon". In 1955, he opened "Music City" a completely stocked music retailer in Hamburg-Steindamm.

As the company continued growing, production was moved to Maimoorweg 44 in Hamburg-Bramfeld in 1956 and at the same time, a new company logo was introduced. Karl-Heinz Weimer recognized early on the importance of working with partners.

He therefore became (in 1958) the sole distributor in Germany for the Swedish accordion and guitar manufacturer Hagström and the Italian electronics manufacturer Binson. Later, the American drum manufacturer Slingerland also became a partner.

1950 - 1956   1956 - 1970

For cymbal manufacturers, Trixon had both the American cymbal maker Zildjian and the Swiss company Paiste in his program.

In regards to the former, Bob Zildjian and Karl-Heinz Weimer had already met during the war and a close friendship developed between them. All of the cymbals though, received an additional Trixon engraving (see below).

    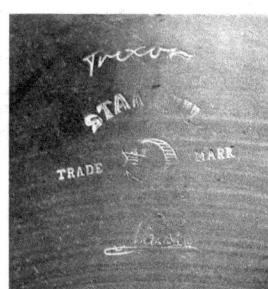

The History of Drums Made In Germany

Karl-Heinz Weimer was also always looking for ways to improve his products.

Included among his many inventions were: a resonant drumhead with a porthole (primarily used for double-sided bass drums), a cymbal arm mounted on the bass drum with a swivel holder that allowed for optimal positioning, tilting and movability and stands with spring mechanisms for the integrated stabilizing feet (click clack, ruck-zuck).

Unfortunately, Weimer lacked both the time - and money - to have most of his ideas patented and therefore, they were soon overtaken by other manufacturers and today are part of the common drum making property. Nevertheless, Trixon can still claim to have been one of the most innovative companies of its day.

Karl-Heinz Weimer had already opened the second pillar of his enterprise in 1955 in Hamburg near the St. Pauli Reeperbahn. When "Music City" relocated directly to the Reeperbahn in 1965, it was 700 square meters in size, which made it one of the largest music stores in Germany.

Over the next years, demand increased and individual production areas, for example tripod construction, were outsourced. At this time, the list of endorsers was already very long - thanks in part to Weimer's unceasing efforts. He visited jazz bars, concert houses and broadcasting station orchestras and successfully convinced musicians there of the quality of his instruments.

Ad Arbiter UK 1967

The big international names were repeatedly invited for guest performances by the broadcasting agencies sponsored by British and American forces occupying Germany at that time (BFN, AFN, RIAS). That's how Weimer was able to win over musicians like Lionel Hampton, Duke Ellington, Big Owen Fletchit, Kenny Clarke, Phil Seaman and Alan Ganley. Even the legendary Buddy Rich agreed - albeit briefly - to do an endorsement. The house set at the Star Club was a Trixon "Luxus Set" and Ringo Starr accompanied the Beatles on it in 1962.

The story goes that after Ringo returned to England, he went to "Drum City" in London to buy a black Trixon. Since they didn't have one in stock, he bought a Ludwig Black Oyster instead. Just imagine how Trixon's history - and that of all other drum manufacturers would have been different if Ringo had actually left "Drum City" with a Trixon ...

Despite this, Trixon was successfully represented on the English market in the first half of the 1960s (it was the time of the British beat boom). The most popular model there was the classic Luxus set with blue-striped wrap.

In 1965, the Chinese military ordered 1000 marching drums which meant production had to work extra shifts. Weimar insisted that he had no idea what had put the Chinese onto him. It is, though, a strange twist in drum making history, especially in light of the fact that today, there are almost no drums at all that don't come from China.

Trixon had already tried in the 1950s to get its foot in the door of the US market. Success, though, first came in 1963 when the St. Louis Music Supply Co. took over distribution there. High demand in the USA led to the decision to expand the factory. In the spring of 1966, production moved to four new 1000-meter large production halls in Hamburg-Reinbek (Liebigstraße). At peak times, 140 workers were employed.

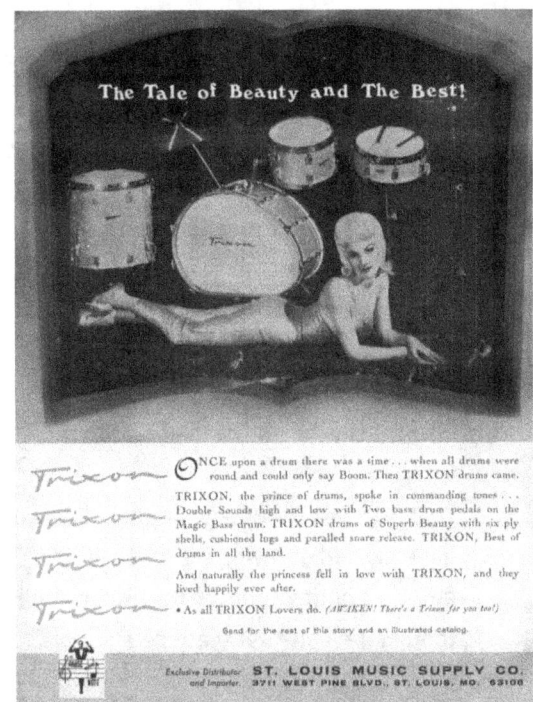

Ad USA 1965

In 1967, Karl-Heinz Weimer made the fateful decision that at first looked very promising but later turned out to be the company's downfall. At this time, unemployment was extremely high in Ireland and foreign companies were being offered investment incentives if they agreed to relocate there.

Karl-Heinz Weimer entered into a joint-venture to produce his drums with the Dutch piano factory Rippen, which had also settled in Ireland. Interconnections between Rippen and the organ manufacturer Thomas Organ Co., which also distributed VOX Instruments, led to Trixon also being sold in the USA under the VOX name for a short time (1967). To avoid conflicts with the St. Louis Music Supply Co. that was continuing to distribute Trixon products, the "Speedfire" was renamed to "Telstar", the "Luxus" changed to "Thunderbolt" and the "Telstar" to "Fanjet". Improperly calculated import tax and shipping costs quickly led to the first problems arising with the Irish production. At first, production in Hamburg continued, but it was planned to phase this out and leave only Service and Administration there. Around 1970, Rippen declared bankruptcy and production came to a halt. Both companies were forcibly placed under state control.

Weimer at first tried to transfer the entire production back to Hamburg, but 70 percent of the machinery and the majority of the necessary components were stuck in Ireland. To get them back, Weimer would have had to go through a lengthy legal battle and then pay back all the incentives that had been paid.

This situation - and the beginning of the "invasion" of much cheaper Japanese drum sets - led Weimer to the decision to stop manufacturing drums and focus his energies on the retail shop "Music City" in Hamburg.

The History of Drums Made In Germany

At first, a handful of employees remained working in Hamburg-Bergedorf to handle maintenance and service. A few individually constructed sets were also made – as far as components were available. The remaining stock and machines were stored in an old school for over 25 years.

Shortly before his death on December 26, 1997, Weimer sold the licensing rights to all these remaining parts and machines to Artur Oeschger, who was hoping to bring the brand back to life. But various problems were then followed by a fire in 1998 that destroyed this dream. Oeschger himself died just two years later after suffering from a serious illness. This also meant the end of the line for Trixon.

That, at least, is how it appeared at first. But recently, new Trixon sets have started showing up on American internet platforms that are (allegedly) a continuation of Karl-Heinz Weimer's philosophy. A quick look, though, reveals that these sets are of Chinese production and the classic Trixon badge has just been glued on. This appears to be, after Rogers, Leedy and Slingerland, just one more attempt to exploit one of the big names in drum making history.

Obtaining replacement parts works quite well though, due largely to the efforts of Ingo Winterberg and his platform: www.trixondrums.de. Interestingly enough, Remo USA still has replacement parts for the unusual "Speedfire" models.

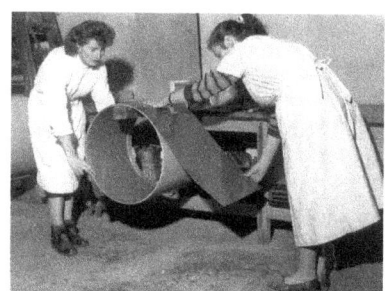

In the 1950s Trixon instruments: (Hand) Made in Germany

As I mentioned at the beginning of this chapter, Trixon is extremely popular with collectors. Prices for its drum sets are higher than those of any other German manufacturer –Sonor included. While sets from other German manufacturers in the 1950s and 1960s can be had for only a few hundred euro, a Trixon Set in the right color can bring around 1500 euro.
Those interested in learning more about this wonderful German manufacture should make sure to check out the book by Ingo Winterberg and his co-author Martin Grimsel "Trix on Trixon - The Story of the German Drum Company". You can find it under: www.trixondrums.de.

TRIXON

Model Overview

The variety and types of models offered during Trixon's entire production lifespan was kept relatively clear and "user-friendly". Model names like "Luxus" or "Swing" always designate a particular setup of individual components and remained the same during the entire production time. For example, the classic combination of bass drum, rack tom, floor tom and snare drum was always sold as "Luxus 0/200".

One could also choose between various bass and snare drum models at no extra charge (according to the catalog). At the end of the 1960s, the configuration of bass drum, two mounted toms, floor tom and snare drum was increasingly accepted as the contemporary drum set of choice. Interestingly, this configuration appeared only once in a Trixon catalog designed for the American market. Other providers already had corresponding models on the market.

In 1967, Trixon drums were also sold in the USA under the brand name VOX.

»Super 0/100« catalogued early 1950s

»Luxus 0/200« »VOX Thunderbolt« catalogued early 1950s > 1970

»Solist 0/300« catalogued early 1950s > 1970

»Swing 0/400« catalogued early 1950s > 1970

»TopStar 0500« catalogued 1967 > 1970

»BigBand 0600« catalogued 1967 > 1970

»Speedfire 0/700-1« catalogued 1961 > 1970

»Speedfire 0/700-2« catalogued 1961 > 1965

»Speedfire 0/700-3« catalogued 1961 > 1967

The History of Drums Made In Germany

Trixon

Model Overview

»Speedfire 0/700«
»Thunderbeat Special« (USA)
»VOX Telstar«
 catalouged 1956 > 1970

»ShowStar 01000«
 catalogued 1967 > 1970

»Model 02000 Telstar«
»VOX Fanjet«
 catalogued 1962 > 1970

»Radio Combi 0/500«
 catalogued early 1950s

»Double Tom Outfit 2490« (USA)
 catalogued mid 1960s

»Junior 0/800«
 catalogued 1960 > 1961

»Mambo 10/000«
 catalogued 1956 > 1960

»Latin-American-Combi 0/600«
 catalogued early 1950s > late 1950s

»Trommelklavier«
 never catalogued

TRIXON

»Speedfire 0/700« Photo 1956

Like no other product, the "Speedfire-Set" is a synonym for this company. It had an elliptical bass drum with two chambers that could be played with two pedals. Five concert toms were racked on it according to size with the largest on the right and the smallest on the left. The snare drum was mounted directly on the bass drum with a clamp arm. Here is one of the first "Speedfire-Sets" from 1956.

When the model "Telstar" with its conical shells was introduced to the market in circa 1962, it was at first called simply "Model 2000". Somewhat later, the name "Telstar" appeared in the catalogs. Up until 1964, the bass drum and stand tom had the same size. The stand tom was played on the 16" side and the bass drum on the 20" one. With the introduction of square lugs in 1964, the stand tom shrank to 16" x 14" x 16" and the larger side was turned to the top.

The concept of sound compression states that the conically formed kettle causes the sound waves to be compromised after they leave the batter head. This in turn generates a much stronger swing on the resonate head that creates a more explosive sound.

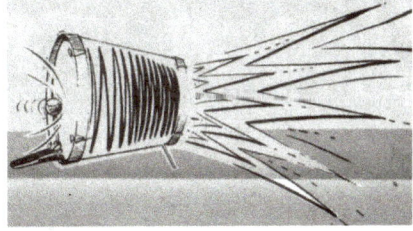

»Telstar Modell 2000« 1962 > 1964

»Telstar« 1965

The History of Drums Made In Germany

»Luxus 0/200« 1954

The "Luxus 0/200" is the absolute standard set (20", 22" or 24" bass drum, 14" snare, 13" rack tom, 16" stand tom) and is surely the most-sold Trixon set - even when its conventional shells seem a bit common when compared to the "Speedfire" and "Telstar".

Another interesting set is the "Mambo" with its central Lionel Hampton attraction tom (with three solid racks for the legs that made it possible for Lionel to dance on it) and concert toms racked around it.

Trixon preferred to use celluloid wraps from the German Celluloid Factory in Speyer for its drum finishes. Trixon was also quite daring when it came to experimenting with colors. Wraps used included:
pearls, sparkles, stripes (applied vertically and horizontally) and moiré wraps (Satin Flame).
The croco wraps are most likely one of a kind.

The shells were triple-layered, then six-layered and made of beech with reinforcement rings in metric sizes until the start of the 1960s.

Heads made from natural skins were used until 1957, when synthetic heads from Remo became more common. The heads were then additionally imprinted with the Trixon name.

Teardrop lugs were used until 1963 when, in general, the design preference changed to using square lugs and these were the first to have plastic underlays.

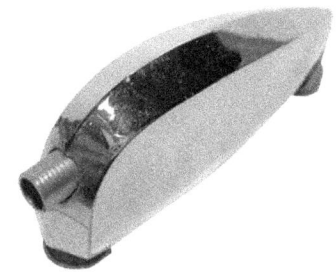

> 1963

1963 > 1964   1965 >

TRIXON

Even today, enthusiasts rave about the form of the large lug screws on the bass drums! The drums' metal rims were bent inwards until 1965. Starting in 1966, they were bent outwards in keeping with the international standard.

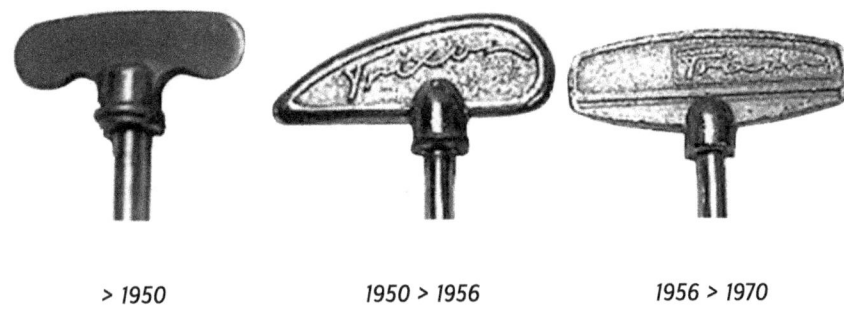

> 1950   1950 > 1956   1956 > 1970

There were numerous pedal models, but the now quite rare "Speedmaster" stands out and is worthy of particular note.

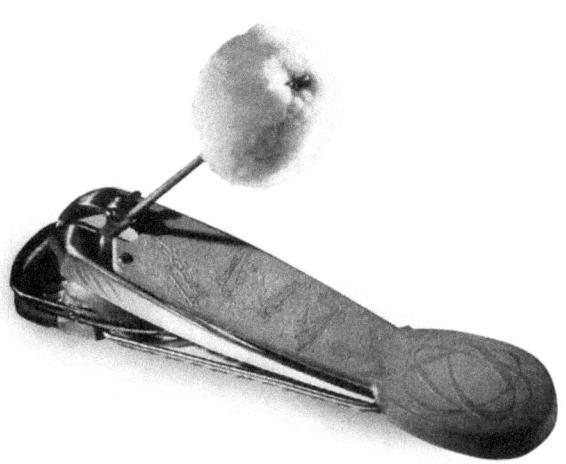

»Speedmaster« Pedal 1954 > 1960

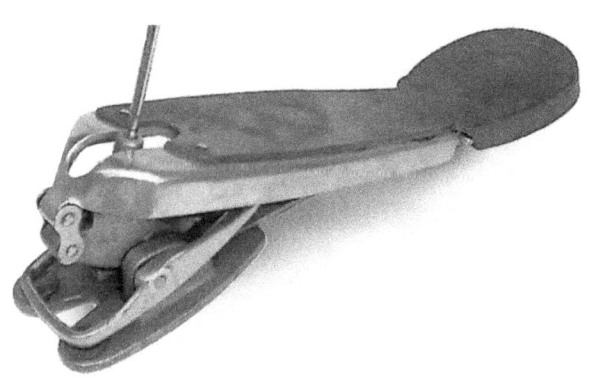

The History of Drums Made In Germany

The History of Drums Made In Germany

Karl Rimmel Schlagzeugbau
Leubas bei Kempten/Allgäu
1946 - 1960

Whereas Trixon was based in northern Germany, our journey now takes us way down south to Kempten in Allgäu where the companies Deri and later Rimmel had their businesses.

The founder of these companies, Karl Rimmel, was born on February 6, 1905 in Diepholz. After finishing school, he trained as a carpenter.

During the typical year-long journey taken by new carpenters, he began to play the accordion using a new system of notes. One year later he was giving lessons himself and leading a group of musicians. Their first official concert in 1931 was a huge success. On November 7th of the same year, he received his accordion teaching certificate in Trossingen and began giving lessons in Allgäu.

1946 > 1960

His first groups were in Immenstadt, Lindenberg and Kempten. In 1933, Karl Rimmel founded an accordion dealership in his hometown of Diepholz. This relocated to the Landhaus on the Residenzplatz in Kempten on October 13, 1935 and here, Rimmel continued to give lessons. During WW II, it became increasingly difficult to operate his business because his most important supplier, the company Hohner, had been put into war materials production.

On July 19, 1944, Kempten was almost completely destroyed by bombs.

Karl Rimmel

In 1946, Karl Rimmel started a music supply shop that carried all instruments and included a workshop for repairs. He soon had suppliers for almost every kind of musical instrument. But he still needed to find a source to produce drums for the region. He joined up with Max Deibel, a former instrument maker from Grasnitz who was already constructing drums there, and they began producing drums in a bicycle work shop at Reichsstraße 5 in Kempten.

This production company was named Deibel & Rimmel after its founders and called DERI. On September 19, 1949 Rimmel applied for a patent at the German Patent Office for a drum shell made of ordinary beech plywood that was supposedly fireproof. They manufactured the shells and rims out of beech and bought hides for the drumheads from various farmers on the river Iller. The skins then had to be cleaned in a tedious process using alum.

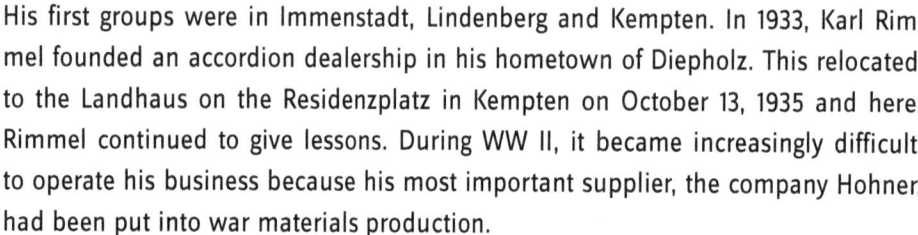

The metal work took place in Munich where at this time, mainly polished aluminum casting and later nickel plated brass casting were used.

Tripods and cymbals were at first purchased separately in Munich from Korn & Riedel (Korri - see page 97).

In 1954, the retail division moved to the Kempten Lingstraße.

42

DERI

The occasion of the 1000th drum: Karl Rimmel (right) and Max Deibel (2nd from right) with employees

On May 24, 1955, Karl Rimmel applied for a new patent – this time for a pedal where the foot plate was connected to the beater's shaft with elastic spring steel.

Reinhard Wranizka remembers that the machine functioned well, but with time, the spring steel tended to break.

Rimmel had an inner circle of friends and employees around him right from day one. In addition to Deibel, these included Heinz Meinlschmidt, Reinhard Wranizka, Franz Ambrosch (who would later take over the retail trade), Rudi Grusche and Georg Kamm.

A win in the lottery by this group made it possible for Rimmel to purchase a carpenter's shop in the Leubas part of Kemptener in 1957. He expanded production with the addition of metalworking and galvanization shops.

Reinhard Wranizka was instrumental in the build-up of this area and here, all metal components could now be manufactured and processed and no longer had to be sent to Munich for chroming.

Max Deibel died at the beginning of the 1960's and the Deri emblem soon vanished from the drums. Now the products were simply called Rimmel, but more about that in the next chapter.

The "Dixi" was a DERI drum that included an elliptical bass drum in the program. It is often confused with the "Trixon Speedfire", but as opposed to it, the "Dixi" features an asymmetrical ellipse and two bass drum chambers separated by a plate.

Frankfurt music fair 1957

43

The History of Drums Made In Germany

Another distinctive feature in the DERI product palette is the so-called "case drum" that was devised by the Rimmel employee Heinz Meinlschmidt. To quote him, "Back then, I was playing a lot of dance music and the fact that I had to carry around so many cases really bothered me. So I cut the bass drum in half and tongue and grooved it. Then I could put the smaller drums and stands inside it and save a lot of space."

In addition to drums and hardware, the product palate at the end of the 1950's already included bongos, timbales, conga-like drums, timpani, field drums, fanfare horns, small percussion instruments, sticks and mallets as well as bum basses (bladder fiddles).

The DeRi Dami Drumset

In an interview from March 1984, the famous composer Karlheinz Stockhausen reported that he went to a fair in 1960 in Frankfurt and found a drum made by Karl Rimmel called a "kidney drum" that he used in his work "Momente", premiered on the 21st of May 1962 at WDR in Cologne.

In the 1950s, Latin American music became extremely popular in Germany, which also affected the range of percussion instruments offered by manufacturers. Bongos were integrated into many sets and the Deri "Dixi" and the Trixon "Speedfire" with a whole battery of concert toms were also due to this new style of music. The disadvantage of these sets was that they were difficult to assemble and transport. That's exactly what this set with its original name "Dami" was to make things easier. In the center stood a kidney-shaped drum. It provided the sound of multiple tom toms and a bass drum played from below by a redirected pedal. Their two natural heads were tuned on each side using 16 lugs, which were at different distances, depending on the curvature of the drum. An oval shaped snare drum nestled into its indentation. There were also mounts for two cymbal arms and snare drum attached to it.

Karlheinz Stockhausen himself said about the glissando drum: "It has a size of about, I would say, 31/2 feet long but is kidney-shaped, and it stands on four metal legs. It is built like a tom-tom but has as witch for being half-muted or completely muted. It has several in-between steps of muting that are discontinuous. And the drum has this incredible quality that enables you to produce a 11/2 octave glissando by moving from the center (the largest diameter of the drum) toward the edge (the smallest diameter of the skin). The drum has two calf skins, upper and lower. I still have several kidney drum skins at home. This drum is extraordinarily beautiful in all qualities that concern the focusing of the sound, the timbre. It sounds like one of the best timpani, if you like. With a wooden stick-on-stick rim shot while moving one stick you get this marvelous overtone glissando which goes from the highest [e] to the [u] sound and at the same time when you draw up the left stick (let's say the stick that is underneath and touching the rim), if you draw it over the whole skin from the center to the edge,

Das erste Werbebild eines Prototypen für die Frühjahrsmesse in Frankfurt zeigt noch deutlich mehr Spannböckchen als spätere Modelle.

you get a 11/2 octave glissando. When you have a series of attacks from the center of the skin going to the edge, this same glissando is produced. There is also a continuous glissando possible with a roll, and in addition, the basic skin tension is even tunable. Now, Momente has been composed for that drum, and my works which are slightly complex in performance practice are not performed very often. « (Interview by Michael Udow, March 1984)

The oval snare was also used in the piece "Momente", but mounted individually on a snare stand, as can be seen from the score. But the company failed to get many customers interested in this set up and so it was discontinued shortly after it was introduced. It probably never appeared in a catalog. When "Momente" was to be performed again in 1969, Stockhausen ordered some more of these drums, which was quite difficult because a fire in the factory destroyed the original templates for building the kidney shell. Therefore, these later drums vary slightly from the originals in shape and size. They also don't have mounts for the add-on parts because Stockhausen was only interested in the kidney drum itself.

Today there are still a couple kidney drums at the Stockhausen foundation as well as one that is stored at WDR. About five other drums are known to be in the hands of private collectors.

The History of Drums Made In Germany

RIMMEL

The History of Drums Made In Germany

Karl Rimmel Schlagzeugbau
Leubas bei Kempten/Allgäu
1960 -1980

Karl Rimmel had founded the Deri Company with Max Deibel in 1946. But after Deibel's death at the beginning of the 1960's, the DERI emblem soon disappeared from the drums. The products were now known only by the name RIMMEL, even though up to the end of the 1960s, many drums had no badges at all.

instruments
1960 - 1995

In addition to retailing music instruments, producing drums and metal processing, Rimmel discovered a new sector: manufacturing synthetic heads.
He had been experimenting with the idea since the end of the 1950s. The question of who first discovered synthetic heads remains controversial. The company Evans continues to claim this honor for itself. This does speak to the facts, in so far as Evans had the first synthetic heads that actually functioned both technically and commercially. But before Chick Evans, there were others experimenting in various places around the globe with alternative drumheads. For example, there are patent documents from the early 19th century for heads made of two-ply linen soaked in a water-resistant substance, as well as a method that used a thin metal coating.
In the end, courts came to the conclusion that several inventors working independently of each other had the same idea at the same time.
A further question of interest is: what happens after the heads are mounted? After all, once the head is placed on the drum and tightened, it can be subject to tension of 1000 kilos and more.
Two methods are primarily used here:

1. The film is placed in a metal hoop and effused with cast resin.
The German company RKB (Reichelsheimer Kunststoffbetriebe Dingeldein & Grosh OHG) applied for a design patent for it in 1961 and this method is still favored by the company Remo.

2. The film is wound around a rod and the two are mechanically interlaced against each other. Ludwig applied for the patent for this process in the USA in 1959 and still uses this method.

Karl Rimmel applied in 1961 for patents in Germany, France, England and Switzerland und marketed them under name "Stabil". His method varied in that the film was additionally pressed into the ring.
Bill Ludwig II wrote a letter to Karl Rimmel, in which he threatened to take legal action. Nothing came of this though, because in the mid 1960s, an American court ruled that the method had already been used previously to install train windows (and in part attachment processes for sieves and lamp shades).

RIMMEL

The company Rimmel increasingly focused its activities on metal finishing, and at the start of the 1960s, was purchasing drum shells from Sindelfinger Holzringen (marching) and from Sonor (drum sets). As Rimmel enjoyed an excellent reputation for its metal work and processing, it in turn supplied more and more instrument manufacturers with metal products.

Up until Rimmel's closing, there was most likely no drum manufacturer in Germany that hadn't used some type of metal part supplied by Rimmel. The company also increasingly delivered to other branches, such as bicycle and automobile manufactures.

The Rimmel drums manufactured in the 1960s stand out through their attractive lug design, good chrome quality and beautiful surfaces. A bestseller was the starter set "Micky" that was sold under the house name and also under various other names by mail order chains. Rimmel drums were also sold under brand names like Blackfield or McEvans.

»Micky« (catalogued 1975)
bd 20"x 10" - sn 13"x 4" - tt 11" - ft 14"

Learner drum "First Step" (catalogued 1975)
bd 18"x 10" - sn 12"x 4" - tt 11"x6"

»Playmaster 312« (catalogued 1975)
bd 20"x 14" - sn 14"x 5" - tt 12" x 8" - ft 16"x 16"

»Playmaster 512« (catalogued 1975)
bd 22"x 14" - sn 14"x 7" - tt 12" - tt 13" - ft 16"x 16"

The History of Drums Made In Germany

Rimmel
»Professional 612«
(catalogued 1975)
bd 22"x 14"
sn 14"x 6"
tt 12"x 8"
tt 13"x 8"
ft 16"x 16"
ft 19"x 19"

Towards the end of the 1960s, the lug design was changed to a teardrop form similar to the Gretsch lug. This was also when Rimmel used an endorser for the first time. "The Bamboos of Jamaica" were a group of musicians who played all kinds of percussion instruments from Rimmel. One of their members, "Jamaica Papa Curvin," is still highly esteemed in Reggae circles today.

Another endorser was the well-known jazz drummer "Big Fletchit" Campbell, who played Rimmel drums up to his death in 1983.

According to the Allgäuer Newspaper, Udo Jürgens' rhythm group also used Rimmel timpani, at least during one concert in Kempten.

Former Rimmel employees are still outraged today about a huge event in the Ravensburg City Concert Hall where Rimmel logos had to be covered up - but the ones from Sonor were allowed to remain visible.

In 1969, the company also attempted to manufacture cymbals, but as one employee put it, "this didn't work."
But who knows, it certainly served some purpose!

At the beginning of the new century, Karl Rimmel turned 65 and his involvement in the company continuously decreased. In 1974, the businessman Hans Sattler took over management of the metal working, drum construction and head production. He and Karl Rimmel attended the Music Trade Fair in the spring of 1974. It became immediately clear to him that the company Rimmel had no chance of market success with drum production, as this would require more capital being invested in development. Nevertheless, he decided to keep on with drum production for the time being.

Mr. Sattler and Mr. Rimmel in the galvanization shop

New hardware with ball joints and new designs for lugs were developed. The legendary chromed plated rims came into use and were also supplied to Sonor for the Phonic and Signature series. Acrylic sets with the same shells manufactured by Sonor were produced and even the quadratic shells and 8" deep snares were introduced at the beginning of the 1980s. Despite lucrative orders from the armies in the Ivory Coast and Ecuador, for example, Rimmel drums kept losing their share of the market. In contrast, the metal working sector was increasingly successful and delivered mainly to suppliers for Bosch (brakes and injection systems), as well as other automobile industry suppliers.

In 1985, Sattler stopped drum manufacturing for good, but continued to run the metal processing department successfully until 1989. Today, it is part of the Zeschky Group in Wetter.

The head production area was sold to the Westharzer Musikhaus. Since 2020 the production went to St-Drums in Pirmasens. Even today, heads are still being produced on the old machines there. Especially for shells with metric dimensions, this is sometimes the only place to find replacements.
Peter Schätzel from Seeshaupt on Starnberger See and his partner Manfred Bickert bought the drum production machines, tools and raw materials and tried, as Schätzel put it, "to keep the company from dying."

The History of Drums Made In Germany

Company management 1983:
Hans Sattler, U. Eisenak, H. Heimrath, O. Waldhauser

Rimmel factory, Leubas 1983

RIMMEL

These photos show the unusual model "Showman" with its elliptical bass drum and six concert toms.

During this time, Rimmel mainly produced based on customer orders received.
The products were made using Rimmel lugs (Schätzel still has 7.5 tons of them stored today) and shells and hardware from Sonor.

The most illustrious client then was the meanwhile deceased Nazareth drummer Darryl Sweet. During a tour in Germany, he played on Rimmel drums. According to Schätzel, "A friend who was also a musician organized it, but we didn't find out about the tour until three days before it started. He needed two 24" bass drums and six extra-long toms. We worked night and day and brought the set to Augsburg in time for tour begin. By the way, that set was sold a few years ago on Ebay for just a couple of euro."

Music fair 1983 – U. Eisenak, H. Sattler, Karl Rimmel

After Manfred Bickert died unexpectedly, Schätzel stopped drum production. Helmut Hahn from Gunzenhausen took over the majority of the machines and raw materials in the mid 1990s from Peter Schätzel and specializes up to the present in making frame drums and bum basses.

Even though Rimmel always manufactured fine drums, the company never managed to shed its "cheap" image - and this despite the products always ranging in the upper price categories.

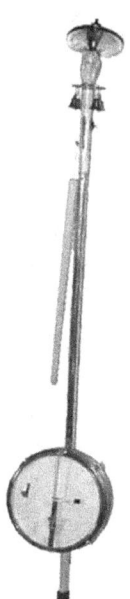

bass/bladder fiddle

The History of Drums Made In Germany

Rimmel, though, has never come close to achieving a cult-status such as Trixon's. Models with well-cared for Sonor shells and very good surface and chrome quality can be bought for a few hundred euro. Replacement part availability is quite good.

After he stopped his work in drum manufacture, Karl Rimmel and his wife Irma continued operating the retail business. In 1978, the business relocated to a 200 square meter premises in the newly completed Kemptner Illerkauf.

On July 1, 1980, Rimmel placed the music shop in the hands of his long-term employee Franz Ambrosch. Today, "Musik Rimmel" is located on the Kemptener Rathausplatz. It is run by Franz Ambrosch's son Manfred Ambrosch and F. Ambrosch's grandson, Klaus Ambrosch, is also following the family tradition and already working in the business.

Manfred Ambrosch

Even after retirement, Karl Rimmel continued to work on new inventions. He applied for patents for an electric barrier for animal stalls and a water-saving mechanism for toilet tanks.

According to the patent for the latter, "This consists of an additional device attached to the water closet that can be pivoted with a swivel lever that in turn, positions a blocking valve that allows water to flow and flush the toilet, but in a lesser amount than when the normal flushing devise is used."
This invention helped not only drummers, but many others as well, to conserve water.

Karl Rimmel died on August 9, 1992. He had no children – but many of his instruments live on ...

»Star 720« (catalogued 1985)
bd 20"x 14"- sn 14"x 6"- tt 12"x 8"- tt 13"x 8"- ft 16"x 16"

»Professional 612« (catalogued 1985)
bd 22"x 14"- sn 14"x 6"- tt 12"x 10"- tt 13"x 12"- ft 16"x 16"

RIMMEL

»8302« 14"x 6" (catalogued 1985)

»8330 H« 14"x 8" (catalogued 1985)

»Black Magic 822« (catalogued 1985)
bd 22"x 18"- sn 14"x 8"- tt 13"x 13"- tt 14"x 14"- ft 16"x 16"

»Playmaster 315 S« (catalogued 1985)
bd 18"x 16"- sn 14"x 6"- tt 12"x 8"- tt 13"x 8"- ft 16"x 16"

The History of Drums Made In Germany

SOME SPECIALS

Trixon wrap samples

The History of Drums Made In Germany

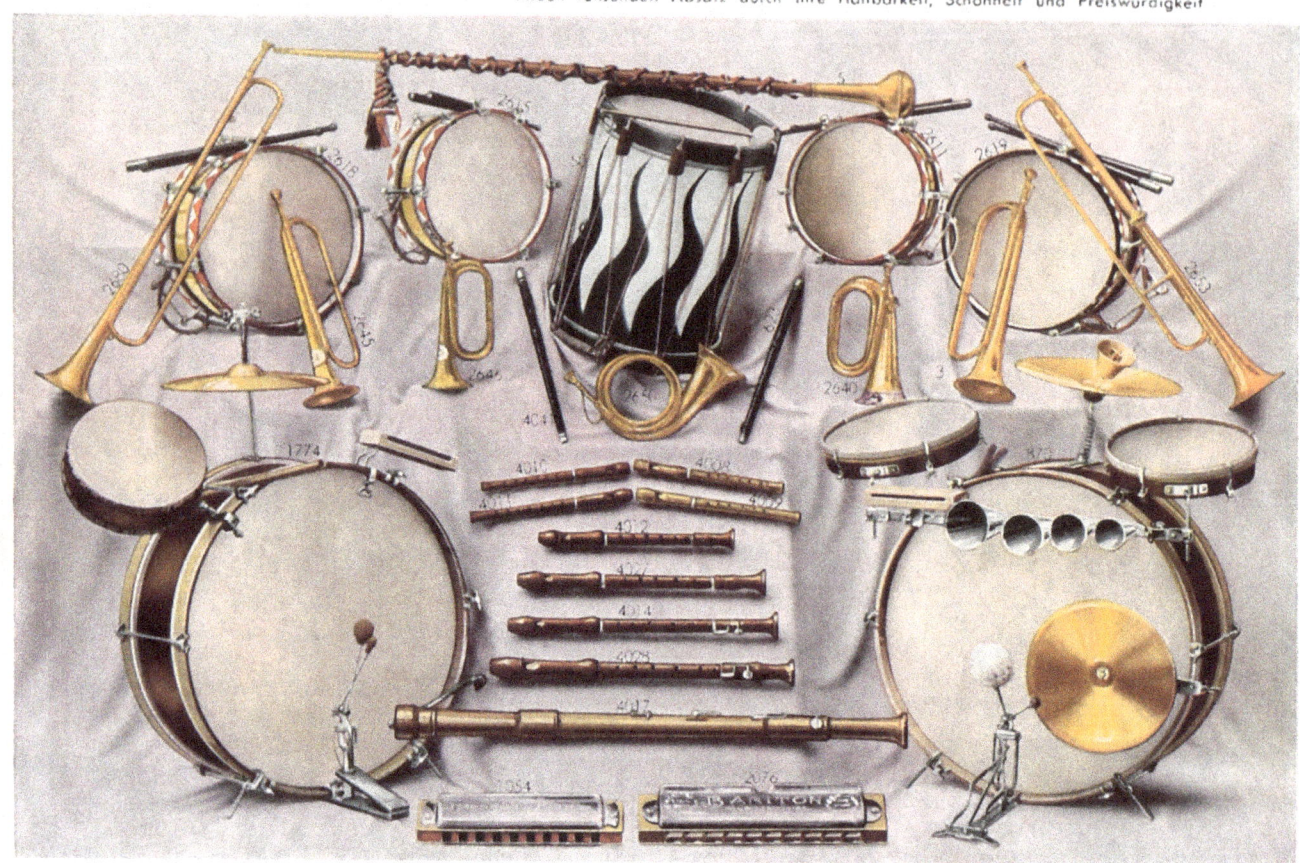

Catalogue shot Meinel & Herold, Klingenthal (Vogtland), ca. 1910

SOME SPECIALS

Sonor Pedals

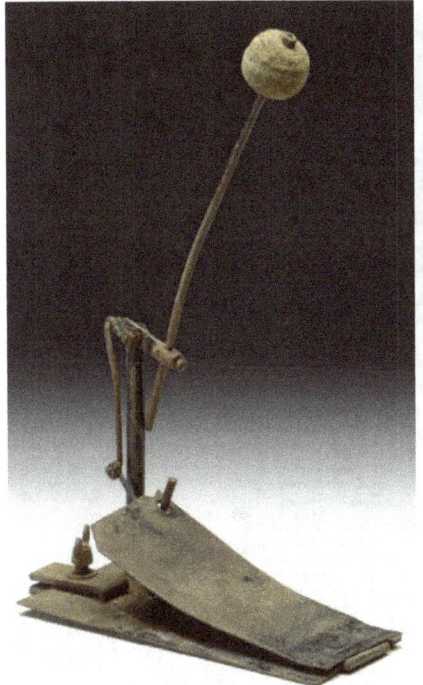

Pedal 1900

Double pedal 1927

Hi-Hat pedal and pedal 1935

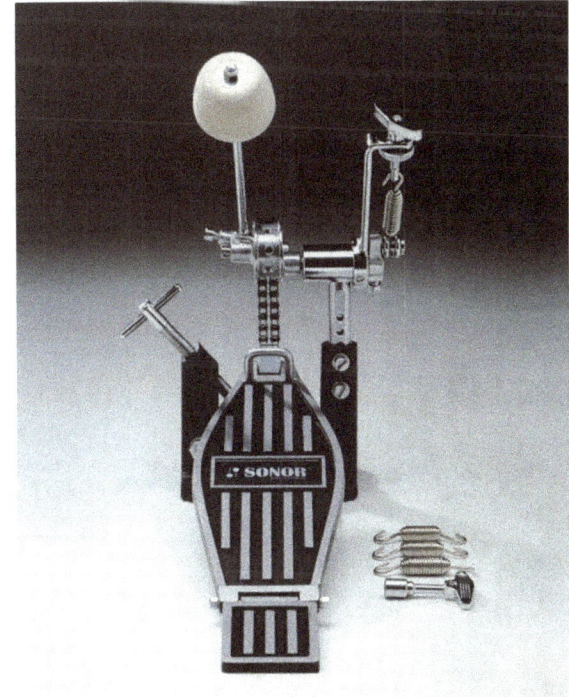

Pedal 1980

Giant Step pedal 2001

The History of Drums Made In Germany

Sonor catalogue 1967/68

Sonor »Champion« 1973

SOME SPECIALS

Sonor »Phonic Soundmachine XK 9212 KS« 1978

The History of Drums Made In Germany

Sonor »Signature« 1982

Sonor »Designer« 1994

SOME SPECIALS

Trixon catalogue cover 1951 (with Teddy Paris)

Trixon promotion ad 1956

The History of Drums Made In Germany

Trixon promotion ad 1962 – Bill Haley and his drummer Dave Holly

Trixon catalogue shot 1962

SOME SPECIALS

Catalogue cover 1964

VOX made by Trixon »Telstar« - 1967

VOX made by Trixon »Fanjet« - 1967

The History of Drums Made In Germany

Lefima catalogue cover 1939

SOME SPECIALS

Rimmel promotion photos 1974

67

The History of Drums Made In Germany

*Rimmel
»Showman 315«
Catalogue 1979*

SOME SPECIALS

Drum Set Supersound 812

- 9251 Baß-Drum 22" x 14"
- 9562 Tom-Tom 16" x 16" mit Dämpfer
- 9551 Tom-Tom 12" x 8" mit Dämpfer
- 9552 Tom-Tom 13" x 8" mit Dämpfer
- 8310 Snare-Drum 14" x 6"
- 5316 Top-Pedal
- 8536 Tom-Tom-Halter
- 9812 Trommelständer
- 9832 Hi-Hat
- 9822 Beckenständer, 2 Stück

orange 478
blau 625
grau 802

Rimmel »Supersound 812« in orange 478 Catalogue 1979

The History of Drums Made In Germany

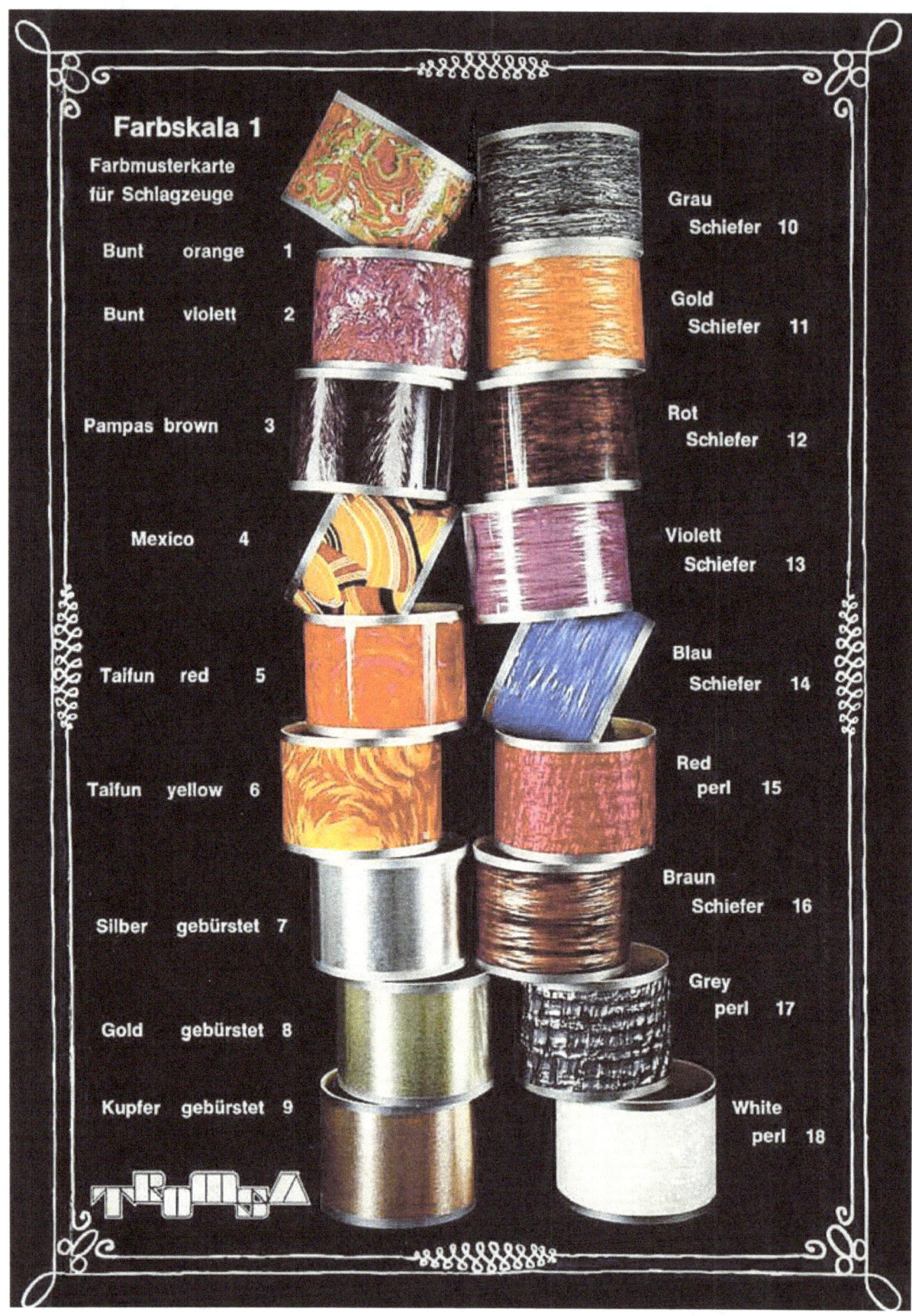

Tromsa color pattern

SOME SPECIALS

Framus catalog cover 1959 with John Ward (Hazy Osterwald-Sextett)

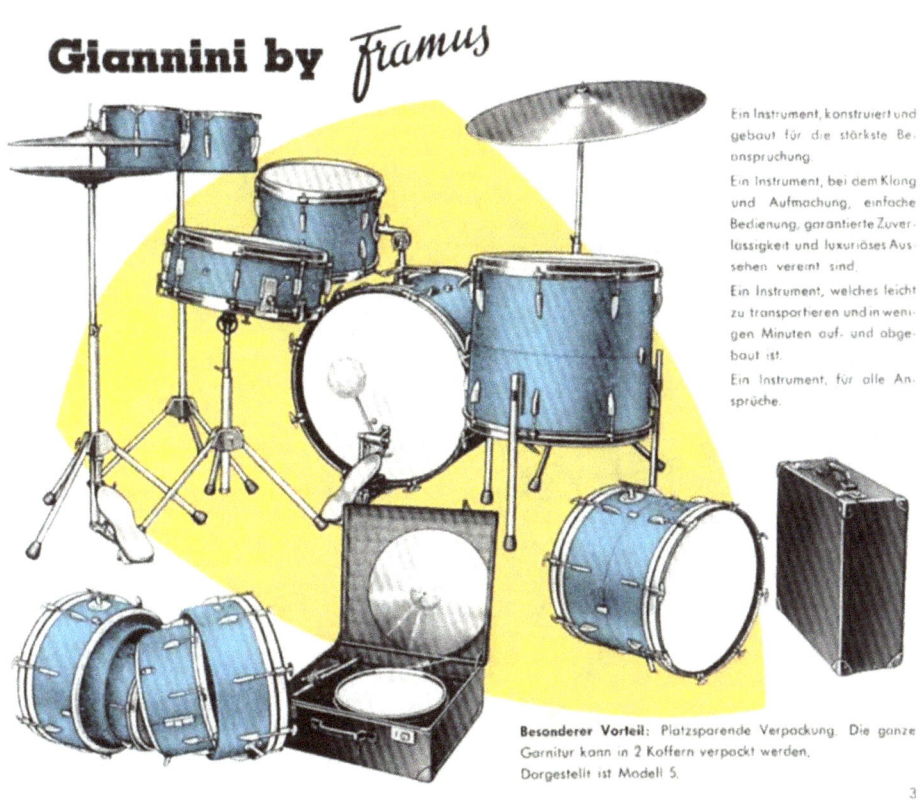

Framus catalogue shot 1959

The History of Drums Made In Germany

Tacton »Modell I« - 1970s

Tacton »Modell II« - 1970s

SOME SPECIALS

Trowa »Duobob« – 1950s

The History of Drums Made In Germany

TROMSA

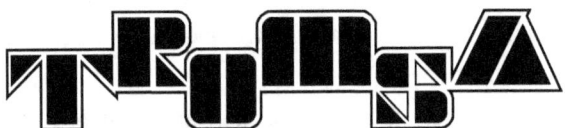

Sattler & Co. OHG
1946 > ~1990

The History of Drums Made In Germany

Just like Rimmel, Tromsa has, unfortunately, been relegated in modern times to the ranks of cheap starter set manufacturers. The early days of both companies began in the 1920s in the city of Graslitz (Kraslice) in what is now the Czech Republic.

1946 > ~1990

Max Deibel, the future partner of Karl Rimmel, as well as Franz Sattler, the founder of Tromsa, began producing musical instruments and their accessories in this city that was traditionally known for its instrument making. At this time, mainly brass instruments, brass drums and cymbals were produced. Even today, the trade of "drum maker" is not officially recognized as a separate profession and drum makers still have the professional designation of brass instrument makers.

It is highly likely that the two men knew each other and perhaps even worked together. The chances of finding anyone still alive who might be able to confirm this are quite slim, though. In 1945, Sattler and Deibel were both forced to leave the Eger area. Many of the displaced instrument makers and dealers settled in Markneunkirchen, in the so-called "Musikwinkel". Deibel, though, made his way to Kempten im Allgäu (see page 44) while fate sent Franz Sattler to Schloss Elberberg/Wolfhagen near Kassel. Around 1946, he started producing drums and drum sets under the name TROMSA (short for TROMmelfabrik Sattler).

Production moved in 1950 to the premises of the former Automobilewerks in Königstädten. Back in the 1920s, this had been an automobile body shop business that in its day produced very luxurious sports cars using chassis from other manufacturers. The company later made agricultural trailers. It declared bankruptcy in 1950 and was then auctioned in a foreclosure sale.

At this time, Tromsa was already delivering percussion instruments for playing light music as well as marching drums, congas, bongos and fronts (special stands that held notes and hid musicians' legs). In 1953, founder Franz Sattler died and his son Hans Sattler took over the company and changed its name and form to Sattler & Co. OHG.

Like most of the other German manufactures at that time, they used thin, cross-laminated beech plywood with reinforced rims for the shells.

The chrome-plated lugs were in the teardrop design. The tom stand rosettes and feet were not chrome-plated and mounted using the characteristic triangle screws. The shells were covered with an unbelievable variety of vibrantly colored, glittery wraps and even a collector occasionally comes across a new one. Tromsa used synthetic heads from the manufacturer RKB (abbreviation for the German company "Reichelsheimer Kunststoff Betriebe, Dingeldein & Grosch").

TROMSA

At the end of the 1960s, the heads were labeled with the Tromsa logo. After RKB discontinued production, heads were acquired from, among others, the company Schmidtgen.

This page shows the drum set from the 1959 catalog. Die Tromsa models were assigned numbers and the one behind the back slash always refers to the amount of drums in the set.

Kombination 802 (catalogued 1959)
bd 22"x 13", sn 14"x 5", tt 13"x 9", ft 14"x 16", ft 16"x 16"

Kombination 711/5 (catalogued 1959)
bd 20"x 13", sn 14"x 5", tt 12"x 9", tt 13"x 9", ft 16"x 16"

Kombination 711/4 (catalogued 1959)
bd 20"x 13", sn 14"x 5", tt 12"x 9", ft 14"x 16"

Kombination 711/3 (catalogued 1959)
bd 20"x 13", sn 14"x 5", tt 12"x 9"

Kombination M4 (catalogued 1959)
bd 20"x 13", sn 14"x 4", tt 10"x 8", ft 14"x 16"

Kombination M3 (catalogued 1959)
bd 20"x 13", sn 14"x 4", tt 10"x 8"

The History of Drums Made In Germany

In the 1950s, the combination with a bongo or timbales set was extremely popular amongst dance musicians who didn't require a lot of equipment.
Tromsa offered the Combination 712.

Hans Sattler only marketed a small part of his product line using his own name. At first, the models' badges were attached with screws and later with glue. But there are many Tromsa sets on the market that either have no badges at all, or ones with names like Roxy, Kings or Concorde (see page 99). This can also be explained by the fact that Tromsa also produced for other music companies and mail order firms.

Kombination 712 (catalogued 1959)
bd 20", sn 14", bongos 7" and 8 ½"

For example, Tromsa made drums for the mail order company Lindberg, the Munich wholesaler Korri (Korn & Richter), the Musikhaus Linek in Hamburg and the Dutch company Frans Papen. Tromsa delivered early sets to the purchasing association used by many German music stores under the name Luxor.

Hans Sattler was once of the first German manufacturers to realize the importance of using the modular or unit construction system that was - and is - also in place by manufactures in the Far East. This system allowed his customers to choose between an entire range of components, hardware and design elements within the existing product lines. Clients then had a customized drum and were able to partially control its price.

Tromsa pedal Z413, catalogued 1959

Just like Rimmel, Tromsa continually built drums with a good sound, but his company as well, was never able to shed its cheap image. Many German drummers started their careers on a Tromsa drum. Nevertheless, the company remained light years away from obtaining the cult status of Trixon.

That's why well-cared for models in their original condition are traded for relatively little money.
In the 1960s, Tromsa made marching drums for Sonor and also made other instruments, such as banjos (jointly with the company Franz Sandner) and ukuleles.

Tromsa pedal Z416, catalogued 1959

TROMSA

Production continued, even though the fluctuating market at the time impacted it negatively, until 1981. Then a huge fire brought production to a standstill for almost an entire year.

Owner Hans Sattler died in 1983 and production was kept up until his partner Karl Kailbert died in 1990. The heirs liquidated the company and sold its buildings and machines. Today, nothing is left to remind us about this important part of German drum making history other than the remaining drums themselves ...

Tromsa Snare Drum K214, 14" x 5" - catalogued 1959

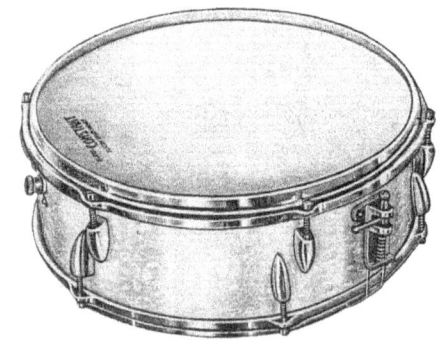
Tromsa Snare Drum K217, 14" x 5" - catalogued 1959

Kombination 802 (catalogued 1979)
bd 22", sn 14", tt 13", ft 16"

Kombination 711/5 (catalogued 1979)
bd 20", sn 14", tt 12", tt 13", ft 16"

Kombination 600/4 (catalogued 1979)
bd 20", sn 14", tt 12", ft 16"

Kombination Amateur (catalogued 1979)
bd 20", sn 13", tt 10" or 12"

The History of Drums Made In Germany

LEFIMA

Leberecht Fischer KG
Since 1861

The History of Drums Made In Germany

Leberecht Fischer KG
Markneukirchen / Cham/Bayern
Since 1861

In addition to Sonor, that looks back on 130 years of tradition and enjoys continuing success today, one other German drum manufacturer still exists and has been making drums even longer than Sonor: the company Lefima in the Bavarian city Cham (Oberpfalz.). According to its company profile, this is the oldest drum production site in Germany. It is also very likely that it is the oldest, still existing drum factory in the entire world! Okay, today it no longer manufactures drum sets, but up until the late 1960s, Lefima was a serious contender in this sector.

Ad 1959

1963

In 1861, Ernst Leberecht Fischer started making drums and tambourines in Markneukirchen in the Vogtland region. The names of the founder and location are reflected in the company name LEFIMA: LEberecht FIscher in MArkneukirchen.
The company won prizes at the World Fair in Paris and at trade fairs in Berlin und Dresden and Lefima then firmly established itself as one of the big players among the many drum makers in the so-called "Musikwinkel" in Markneukirchen/Klingenthal in the Saxon Vogtland.

Ernst Leberecht Fischer

In, 1909 the company's fortunes were placed in the hands of Ernst Albin Fischer, who in turn, passed on the job of running the company to Curt Fischer in 1928.

Ernst Albin Fischer

Curt Fischer

LEFIMA

before 1920

1935

1949

1964

1975

1978

since 2002

The business survived WW I, was completely modernized and the product palette expanded to include timpani, mallets and small percussion instruments. In the 1930s, Lefima was one of the first manufacturers to make a snare drum with carpeting beneath the batter and resonate heads. The demand for drum sets consisting of bass, snare, Charleston machine, toms and cymbals also increased at this time. To keep up with this trend, Lefima henceforth started offering such combinations.

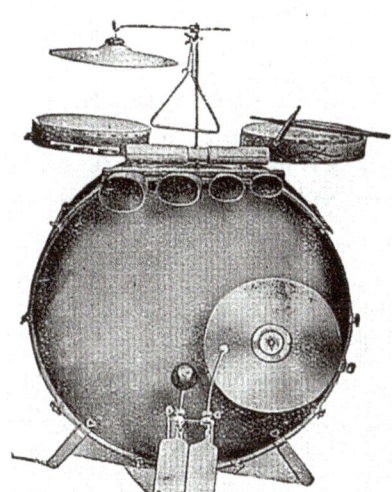

Lefima Modell B No. 15B, Catalog 1939

Lefima Set No. 35/25, Catalog 1939

Lefima Set No. 35/1, Catalogue 1939

Lefima Set No. 35/6, Catalogue 1939

The History of Drums Made In Germany

Shell hardware on earlier Lefima drums consisted of the simplest double lugs positioned centrally.
And in place of lugs, rims were often even tightened using one long tension rod with a screw nut on the bottom side.
In the late 1940s, the lugs still seemed quite bulky - as if fine metal filing had been done on entire metal blocks.
In the 1950s, though, many effective design variations were made to the shapes. Some were round, others teardrop or square, but all of them were of excellent quality. The U-profiles found on the drums with central rivets were not quite

LEFIMA-Schlagzeuge, bestens bewährt bei Funk und Film, Television und Schallplatte, erfreuen uns auch hier bei unserem Doppel-Drums-Solo.
Erich Röner und Fips Fleischer

as elegant, but they were very sturdy and can still be found on many Lefima drums today. The shells (as with almost all German manufacturers) were made of three-ply, cross-laminated beech with two reinforcement rings.

Catalogue shots 1957

In the 1950s, the company also invested in the Orff instrument palette, as well as in early musical education and music therapy.
Because at that time the political situation in (former) East Germany was continuing to worsen, the decision was made to relocate to the present location in Bavarian Charm and risk making a new start.

Lefima contributed numerous innovations to the area of drum sets, including the development of the foot pedal "Rekord" in 1959. It had an incredibly smooth operation considering the circumstances of the day. Drum sets were oriented on what drummers needed back then. They normally included a hanging tom and carried typical names of that time like "Favorit", "Juwel" or "Klub".

The program also featured a quite daring variation with three concert toms in the sizes 6", 8" and 11" on a stainless-steel rack over the bass drum.

Numbered among Lefima's endorsers were well-known drummers who played for broadcasting station dance orchestras such as Günter Kiesant (Broadcast Dance Orchestra Kurt Henkels), Siegfried Möhle (Orchestra Adalbert Lutter) and Thomas Keck (Spree City Stompers).

Günter Kiesant (Orchester Kurt Henkels)

Siegfried Möhle (Orchester Adalbert Lutter)

Thomas Keck (Spree City Stompers)

Karl Heinz Aehnelt

In the mid 1960s, competition was getting tougher due to the appearance of Japanese series products. Attempts were made to remain competitive through use of a budget-model. Although it sported lavish coverings that combined various sparkle wraps, it had chrome-plated, plastic lugs and screw heads on the stands. In 1967, Lefima became the first German manufacturer to completely throw in the towel for this sector. From then on, the company focused successfully on producing concert and marching drums.

In 1981, Karl Heinz Aehnelt (Käthe Fischer's husband) took over the helm at Lefima. His background was with the company Aehnelt Tools. It had been constructing special machines for violin, guitar and brass and wind instrument making, as well as for machinery used to produce automated machines and for the lighting industries since 1924.

Stefan Aehnelt

Since 1997, his son and daughter-in-law, Stefan and Petra Aehnelt have been leading the company.

The History of Drums Made In Germany

Catalogue shot 1957

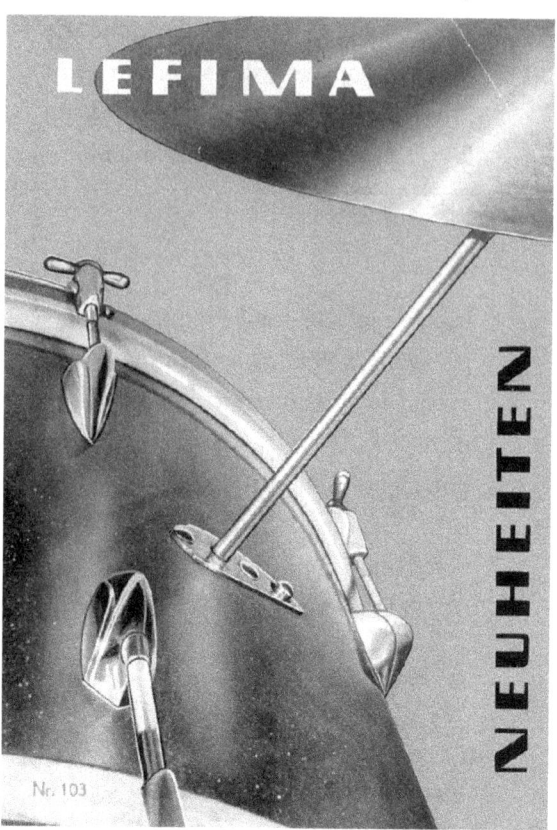

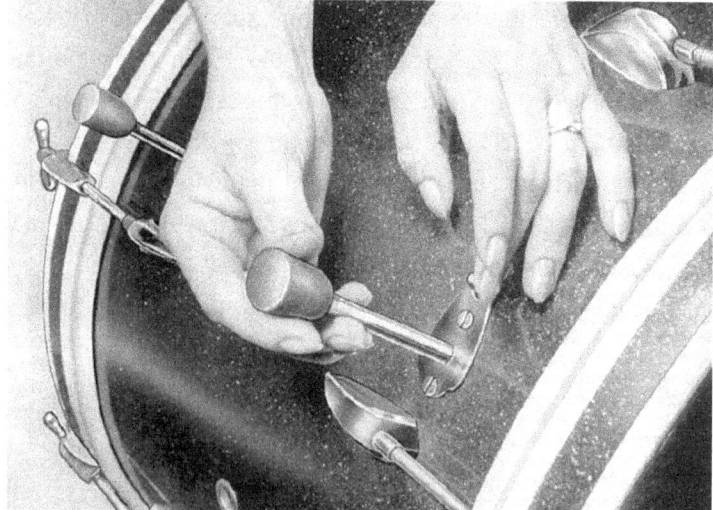

Catalogue shots 1960

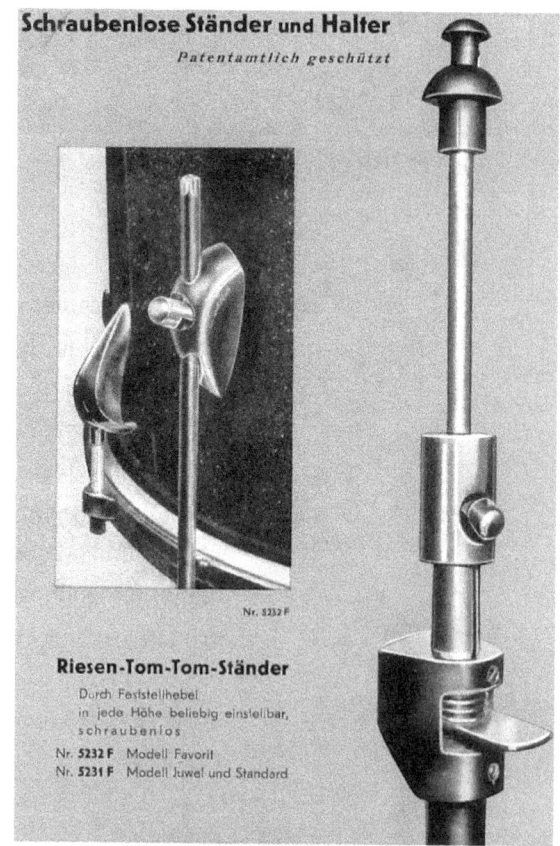

LEFIMA

LEFIMA-JAZZKOMBINATIONEN FÜR ALLE

FAVORIT Nr. 620 F

1 große Trommel Nr. 310, 52×42 cm, eingelegte Reifen,
  incl. 1 Dämpfer Nr. 7203, 1 Beckenhalter Nr. 6556 F, 2 Paar Spitzen Nr. 5905 F
1 kleine Trommel Nr. 153, mit 1 Trommelständer Nr. 2203 F
1 Riesen-Tom-Tom Nr. 1423 mit 1 Ständer Nr. 5232 F
1 dito Nr. 1421 mit 1 Halter Nr. 5501
1 Beckenständer Nr. 5204 F mit 1 Gongbecken 60 cm Ø, Sultan
1 Hi-Hat Nr. 4923 F mit 1 Paar Charlestonbecken 36 cm Ø
1 Zischbecken, 33 cm Ø, Sultan
1 Schlagapparat Nr. 4905

KOLIBRI Nr. 622 F
für die Bar

1 Riesen-Tom-Tom Nr. 1423 mit Innendämpfer
1 Schlagapparat mit Ständer
1 kleine Trommel Nr. 153
1 Trommelständer Nr. 2203 F
1 Beckenständer Nr. 5204 F
1 Gongbecken 60 cm Ø

AMATEUR Nr. 630 F
für das Schulorchester

1 gr. Trommel Nr. 319, 52×42 cm
  incl. 1 Beckenhalter Nr. 6557 F
  3 Stück Spitzen Nr. 5903 F
1 Zischbecken „Sultan", 30 cm Ø
1 kl. Trommel Nr. 206 mit Spiralteppich
1 Trommelständer Nr. 2200 F
1 Riesen-Tom-Tom, 28×23 cm, mit Halter Nr. 5505
1 Schlagapparat Nr. 4908

STANDARD Nr. 625 F

1 große Trommel Nr. 319, 52×42 cm
  2 Paar Spitzen Nr. 5905 F
  1 Beckenhalter Nr. 6557 F
  1 Dämpfer Nr. 7203
1 kleine Trommel Nr. 161
1 Trommelständer Nr. 2203 F
1 Zischbecken, 33 cm Ø, Sultan
1 Beckenständer Nr. 5203 F
1 Gongbecken, 42 cm Ø, Sultan
1 Riesen-Tom-Tom Nr. 1403
  1 Ständer dazu Nr. 5231 F
1 Riesen-Tom-Tom Nr. 1401
  1 Halter dazu Nr. 5501
1 Schlagapparat Nr. 4905
1 Hi-Hat Nr. 4923 F
  1 Paar Becken dazu, 36 cm Ø

KLUB Nr. 627 F

1 große Trommel Nr. 300
  52×42 cm
  eingelegte Reifen
  2 Paar Spitzen Nr. 5905 F
  1 Beckenhalter Nr. 6557 F
  1 Dämpfer Nr. 2703
1 kleine Trommel Nr. 151
1 Trommelständer Nr. 2203 F
1 Riesen-Tom-Tom Nr. 1431
  1 Halter dazu Nr. 5501
1 Zischbecken 33 cm Ø
1 Schlagapparat Nr. 4905

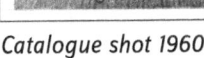

Catalogue shot 1960

The History of Drums Made In Germany

OFFELDER

Offelder Schlagzeugbau
Aachen
1955 - 1975

The History of Drums Made In Germany

Offelder Schlagzeugbau
Aachen
1955 - 1975

This section provides information about a further German manufacturer. Sadly enough, the company Offelder from Aachen has fallen completely into oblivion and is partially unknown even to vintage drum collectors.

Ernst Offelder was born on January 26, 1926 in Reichenberg in Bohemia into a family of musicians. His father was a horn player and his mother a harpist with the Reischenberg Opera Orchestra. His education at the state music school included instruction in violin, piano and horn.

He graduated under the Third Reich special educational regulations and in 1944, became first a drummer with the Reichsarbeitsdienst, (Labor Service), then a soldier. Following his release as prisoner of war, he was hired in 1945 as the second violinist and drummer by the Lebenstadt Concert Orchestra. He played drums for the British occupation in the Bad Pyrmont Casino and at the same time, was a musician at the Thalia Theatre in Hannover and took private lessons from the timpani soloist Hohmann. He joined the Kiel City Orchestra in 1948 as a timpani soloist, and in 1949, moved to the Braunschweig City Theatre. From there, he moved onto Aachen in 1950 and from February 20, 1951 until his retirement, was the city's timpani soloist. This career - combined with family life - would have been more than enough to keep most people fully occupied.

Ernst Offelder, though, also managed to delve into drum and mallet construction. This interest led him to consult, among others, the Swiss drum maker Eugen Giannini. He also had contact with the company DERI in Allgäu.

The question remains, just as with Rimmel and Tromsa, of: what in the world motivated this interest in drum and mallet making?

The likely answer is that after the War, not enough drums could be made and their construction was simpler than that of other instruments.

OFFELDER

In the mid 1950s, he started making drums and mallets in Aachen, first in an attic at Frankenstraße 4 and later, at Adalbertsteinweg 119. At the same time, he also started selling musical instruments in a 35sqm adjoining room and was one of the first dealers of Echolette products in Germany. He and his first wife Gitta Offelder founded the company under the name G. Offelder. They had two children, Ursula und Peter (timpani soloist in the Schleswig-Holstein Symphony Orchestra since 1979).

As with the other German manufacturers, the shells were made out of cross-laminated beech plywood. The streamlined lugs were made of aluminum and finely chrome-plated, and sometimes parts from other manufactures, primarily Trixon, were used.

Offelder advertised in his catalogs that he had the best quality at unbeatable prices due to direct purchase.

His assortment consisted of drum sets with the names Phänoma, Optima, Intima, Exqisit, Multiplus, Perfect, Populär und Piccoletta.

The History of Drums Made In Germany

Similar to the Trixon Speedfire, the combination Supra had five concert toms racked from biggest to smallest, right to left, on the bass drum. The floor tom could also be played using a separate pedal attached below.

Besides drums and mallets, Offelder offered Latin American percussion instruments and fronts that matched the corresponding drum design and color.

The marriage was troubled and ended in divorce. Following it, Gitta Offelder remained head of the mallet production area and expanded it. Both of the children learned the tradition and know-how of mallet making there. The name of the company was changed to Schlägelproduktion Thissen. When daughter Ursula later took over the company, the name was changed again to U. Strasmann and under her leadership, it continues to supply many well-known companies. Son Peter Offelder also makes mallets and his name is quite recognizable in this market sector.

Ernst Offelder closed down drum production in the mid 1970s but kept the music shop up and running. His son from his second marriage, Dirk Offelder, continues to operate that business today at Roermonder Straße 370. Dirk is also a freelance percussionist in high demand. Ernst Offelder's brother Joseph Offelder was also an active percussionist for many years. He was a famous educator and instructor for timpani and drums on the School of Music in Rhineland and at musical training centers in Aachen, as well as a drummer and substitute timpani soloist with the Aachen City Orchestra.

Ernst Offelder died on February 10, 2004.

OFFELDER

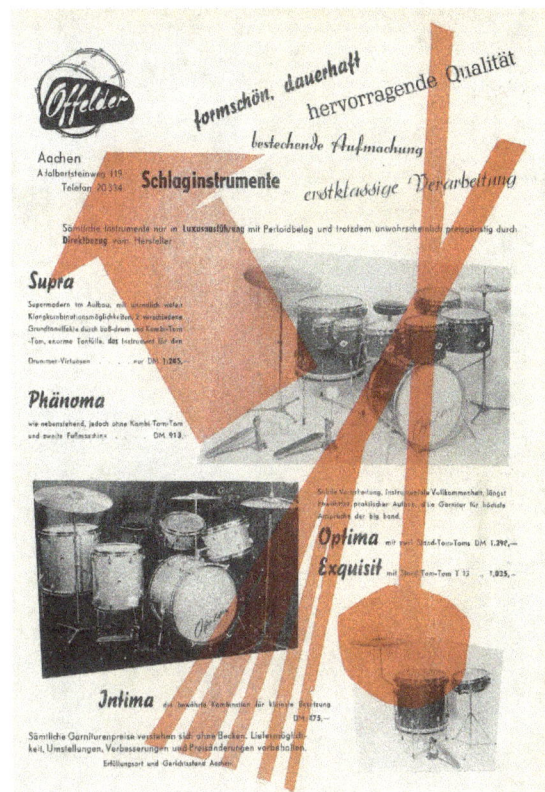

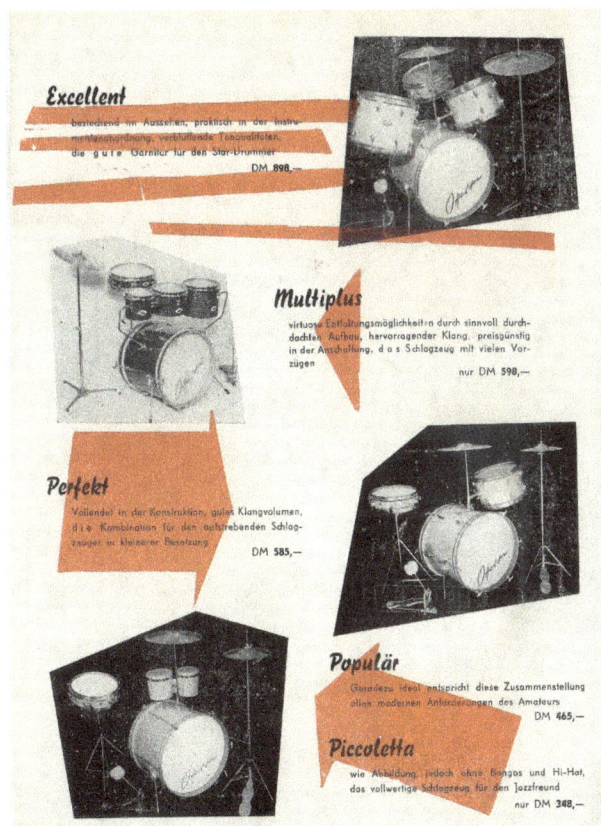

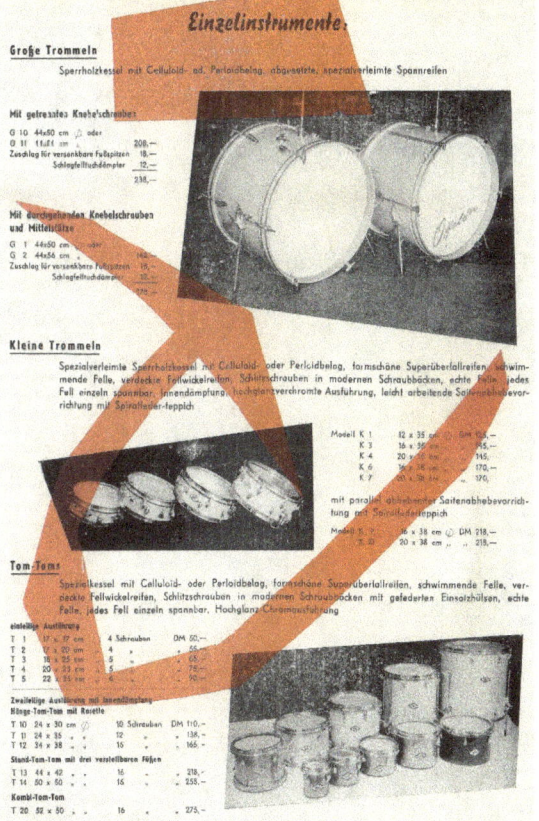

Offelder Catalogue 1967

The History of Drums Made In Germany

KORRI, LINDBERG & CO

Korri, Lindberg & Co

The History of Drums Made In Germany

Up to now, this book has focused on the more or less familiar German drum manufacturers. But there are a few more of them. Some really are smaller manufacturers, while other names are mistakenly considered to be drum makers.

After WW II, instruments were often scarce. That's one reason why especially in rural areas, drums were often also made by carpenters, plumbers and blacksmiths. The goal here was to put together some kind of useable instrument.

The brass instrument makers who, not so long ago, could be awarded the additional title of "Drum Maker," also built the odd drum. They normally purchased shells and rims elsewhere and only lugs - and occasionally strainers - came from the own production and/or were sometimes filed from entire blocks of metal.

Listing all the companies and individuals who made drums remains an impossible task.

In the 1960s, wholesale delivery was so comprehensive and efficient, that it was no longer profitable for many smaller workshops to manufacture their own drums.

At the end of the 1960s, drums produced in the Far East played an ever increasing role. The purchasing association Luxor ordered from Hoshino in Japan. OEM products from Taiwan, like Black Horse or Mark V, soon dominated the mail order catalogs.

Unfortunately, Rimmel, Trixon und Tromsa did not survive this development and Lefima voluntarily got out of the drum making business.

Ad - Jazz Podium 12/1960

Jazz Podium 08/1958

KORRI, LINDBERG & CO

But at the start of the 1980s, drum making took on a new meaning as some manufacturers recognized and acted on the need to make their drums stand out from the crowd of series products on offer.

The most famous supplier here was certainly the company Troyan in Munich. There were others at work here though, even if many of them never got further than building prototypes such as the manufacturer JS Drums in Freiburg. Here is a small selection of some of these companies.

Framus (Franken-Musik, Fred Wilfer K.G. Bubenreuth near Erlangen) included in 1959 the "Giannini by Framas" in order to have drums in its palette of deliverable instruments. There were six different sets on offer. These ranged from a small starter set to the professional "Luxus set" that claimed to meet every possible need. These were all models from the Swiss manufacturer Giannini, but they were produced by Framus in Bubenreuth.

Korri (Korn and Riedel, Music Store and Wholesalers in Feldkirchen near Munich) was a music instrument wholesaler and manufacturer in Munich. Production began here after WW II with cymbals, and stand production and metal processing were added later. In the early days, Rimmel sent its hardware there to be, for example, chrome-plated. The company also imported instruments from the former GDR.

Drums that carry the Korri badge occasionally turn up, but these almost always turn out to be drums made by Tromsa from Königstädten (see page 75).

Framus »Modell 5« with Teddy Paris 1959

The History of Drums Made In Germany

Lindberg was a large music store in Munich. From just after WW II up until the early 1970s, it issued a very successful catalogue for music instruments. Even though Lindberg logos on pedals or drums can make it seem like these are Lindberg products, they were all commissioned and made by various other German manufacturers and had names like "Tanzturnier" or "Jazzkönig".

Luxor is also among the candidates that are often mistakenly taken to be manufacturers. But in fact, Luxor stems from a purchasing association for various German music stores under the overall control of the music store Reisser in Ulm. These retailers bought musical instruments in bulk and labeled them with the name Luxor. This procedure is also known as OEM (original equipment manufacturer) and is still practiced widely today. The company Tromsa was the supplier up to the early 1970s (see page 75).

Nr. 5704 c „Tanztournier"

LINDBERG-Schlagzeug „Jazzkönig" Nr. 5707 c

Roland Meinl founded the wholesale and manufacturing company Meinl in 1951. It first specialized in brass instruments, but soon added cymbals and later, Roland Meinl expanded to include retail products from other brand-name instrument manufacturers. His most important partner for this was the Japanese company Hoshino Gakki with its products Star Drums (from the mid 1970s called Tama) and Ibanez Guitars. Interestingly, around the mid 1960s, Meinl was also the retailer in Germany for Pearl Drums.

Nr. 5707 b „Jazzkönig"

KORRI, LINDBERG & CO

In the 1970s and 1980s there were individual drums from Japan or Taiwan, and an interesting set made of fiberglass that carried the Meinl logo. Today, Meinl is one of the world's top manufacturers of cymbals and percussion instruments.

Meinl drum set made of fibreglass

Müller & Bock was a small drum manufacturer in Bad Canstatt near Stuttgart. Their lugs had a simple design and were very massive. Rims and strainers were purchased elsewhere. Fine details like golden decorative stripes made them stand out from the competition, though.

Music shops like Hack in Göttingen, Lineck in Hamburg or Mollenhauer in Fulda, had their own badges put on drums, or names such as "Roxy" or "Kings". The manufacturer was often the Tromsa (see page 75).

Pückert was a retailer and manufacturer for brass instruments in Bavaria that also produced percussion instruments at the beginning of the 1950s. The lugs had a very square design and were filed out of metal blocks.

RKB (abbreviation for "Reichelsheimer Kunststoff Betriebe, Dingeldein & Grosch") only produced drumheads - but was often mistaken for a drum manufacturer because many Tromsa drums that had been delivered without a logo, had RKB heads on them.

The History of Drums Made In Germany

The drum maker Max Schimmel from Markneukirchen is hidden behind marching drums with the trademark of a mold (Englich for Schimmel). Instruments of high quality came from his workshop until the Second World War.

Troyan in Munich began making drums at the beginning of the 1980s using the stave shell method. At the time, the owner Awerinus "Fex" Rizos was irritated by the non-round shell shapes made by many brand-name manufacturers. He was also bothered by shells that were good – but had bad hardware. So Rizos didn't manufacture own hardware. His customers could pick and choose from various manufacturers and have their drums fitted with the hardware of their choice.

In the mid 1990s, Alex Zachow, took over management and up to the present, is the only official master drum maker in the company.

Ad 1952

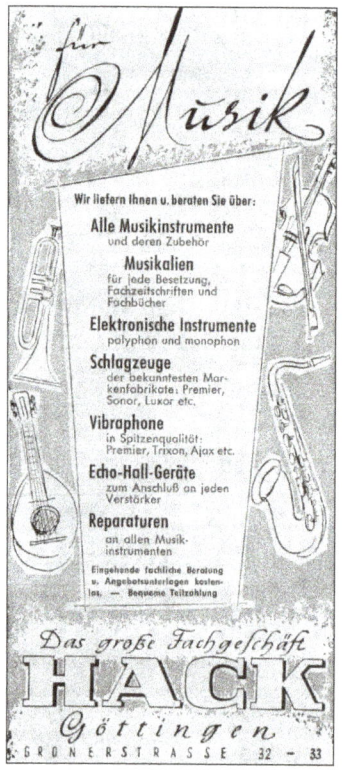

Ad 1960

Mail order companies such as Quelle and Neckermann had drums on offer. Up until the end of the 1960s, these drums were most often from Rimmel and Tromsa. The drums were almost always delivered without badges and had names like "Micky" oder "Dixieland".

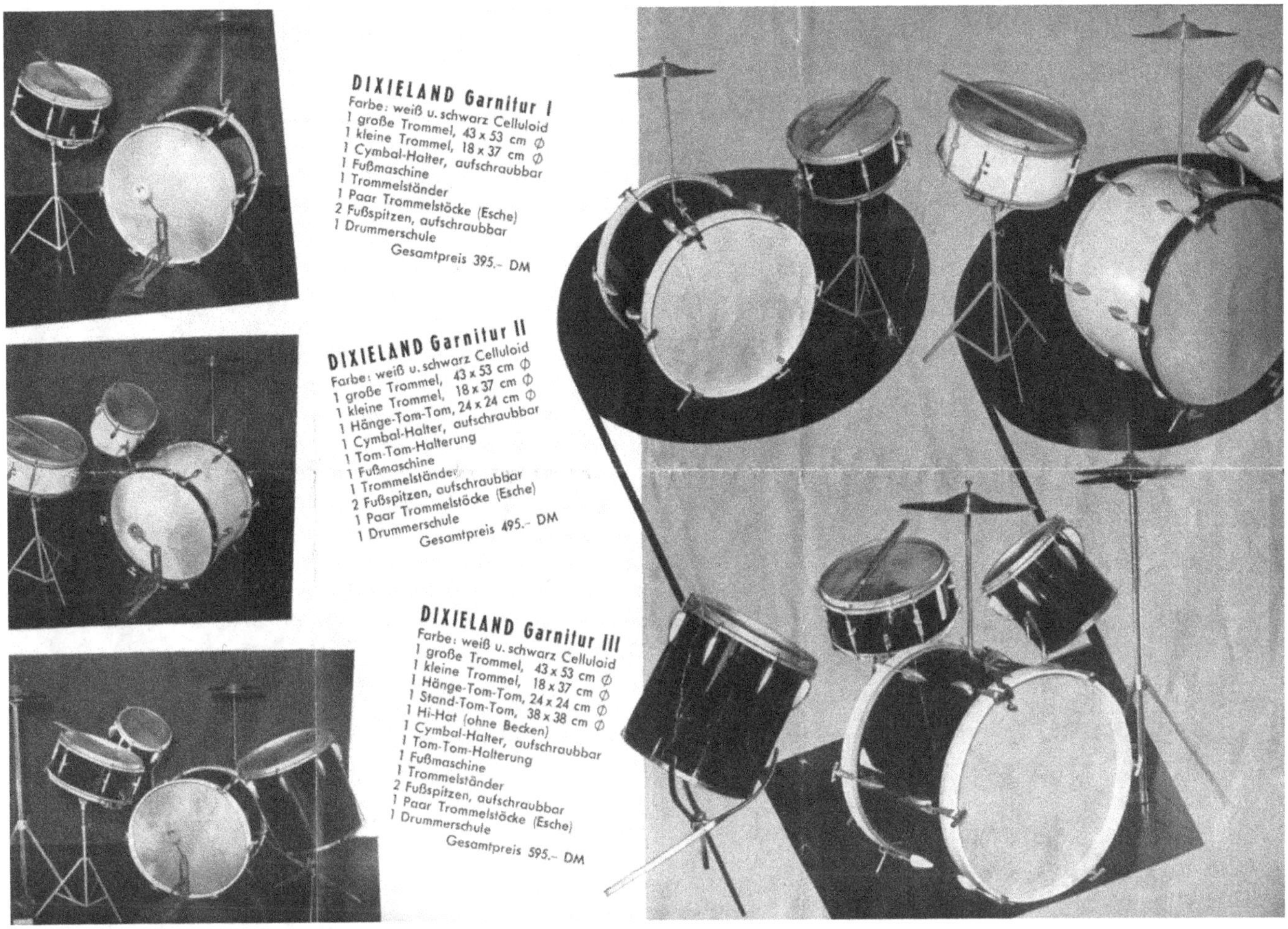

KORRI, LINDBERG & CO

Dixieland catalogue 1950s

DIXIELAND Garnitur I
Farbe: weiß u. schwarz Celluloid
1 große Trommel, 43 x 53 cm ⌀
1 kleine Trommel, 18 x 37 cm ⌀
1 Cymbal-Halter, aufschraubbar
1 Fußmaschine
1 Trommelständer
1 Paar Trommelstöcke (Esche)
2 Fußspitzen, aufschraubbar
1 Drummerschule
   Gesamtpreis 395.- DM

DIXIELAND Garnitur II
Farbe: weiß u. schwarz Celluloid
1 große Trommel, 43 x 53 cm ⌀
1 kleine Trommel, 18 x 37 cm ⌀
1 Hänge-Tom-Tom, 24 x 24 cm ⌀
1 Cymbal-Halter, aufschraubbar
1 Tom-Tom-Halterung
1 Fußmaschine
1 Trommelständer
2 Fußspitzen, aufschraubbar
1 Paar Trommelstöcke (Esche)
1 Drummerschule
   Gesamtpreis 495.- DM

DIXIELAND Garnitur III
Farbe: weiß u. schwarz Celluloid
1 große Trommel, 43 x 53 cm ⌀
1 kleine Trommel, 18 x 37 cm ⌀
1 Hänge-Tom-Tom, 24 x 24 cm ⌀
1 Stand-Tom-Tom, 38 x 38 cm ⌀
1 Hi-Hat (ohne Becken)
1 Cymbal-Halter, aufschraubbar
1 Tom-Tom-Halterung
1 Fußmaschine
1 Trommelständer
2 Fußspitzen, aufschraubbar
1 Paar Trommelstöcke (Esche)
1 Drummerschule
   Gesamtpreis 595.- DM

Roxy drum set of the 1950s/60s

The History of Drums Made In Germany

GDR 1945 - 1990

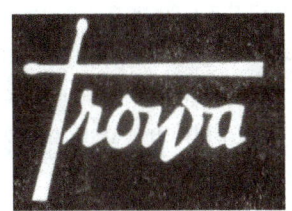 

**Constructions of drums in the GDR
1945 - 1990**

The History of Drums Made In Germany

Constructions of drums in the GDR 1945 - 1990

Chapter four provided a closer look at the company Sonor. To refresh your memory: Otto Link had steered Sonor through the turmoil of WW II and after Germany was divided, the order was given to expropriate the company and arrest the owner. Otto Link barely managed to escape this fate by fleeing the GDR a quite spectacular way. Sonor was taken over by the GDR government and from then on, known as Trowa Instruments, VEB (from the German Trommelwaren – drum products, and volkseigener Betrieb – nationalized company). Throughout its existence, obtaining material would be a huge problem for Trowa. This meant that many good ideas could not be implemented fully – if at all. At first, the former Sonor employees manufactured using the simplest designs just like before the War.

For example, rods were mounted with clips on simply flanged rims, and then later, individual bulky-looking lugs were filed from blocks of metal in the design used at this time for Ludwig lugs.

In the 1950s though, the infant GDR was brimming with confidence and the tone was to develop new products.

The Trowa drums from this time had their own design. The shells were mostly made of plywood, usually beech or whatever could be found at the moment, and were lacquered on the inside in red or gray. The wraps used were of a much different design and quality than those for drums in the West.

The various lugs from the 1950s were quite finely made and stood out through their classical beauty. But soon, the citizens in the GDR were peering across the border and it was decided to produce a copy of the West German Sonor drum with its teardrop lugs.

Trowa »Schlagzeugkombination Duobob«, drum set 1950s

GDR 1945 - 1990

The "Dixie" model with its conical shells really makes one think of the Trixon "Telstar" drum (page 37)

Trowa "Solist" model 1965

The "Mambo" model is almost identical to the Trixon "Mambo" Set (page 36)

Only the tom rack and other add-on parts varied greatly in design and the mechanical parts also didn't work as well as their West German counterparts. Ideas for solving such problems abounded. But some of them, such as the parallel snare strainer, were quite complicated and the lack of material meant they could not be constructed optimally. This was reason enough for musicians in East German - and Eastern Europe - to rebel and instruments for professional musicians were imported from the West.

Trowa "Tournee" model 1965

The "Big Band" combination from 1965 has a lot in common with a Lefima model (page 85)

The History of Drums Made In Germany

Stand at the Leipzig Spring Trade Fair 1967

At the end of the 1960s, a new wave of politically driven self confidence arose which in turn, led to another bout of in-house designs: triangular lugs and round rosettes made of sheet metal suited the shrill atmosphere of the times, but quality remained at the level of starter instruments used in those days. Wraps used came from production in the West.

Starting in the mid 1970s, products were marketed under the brand name "Tacton". The West German importer was the Bavarian company Korri ("Korn & Riedel"). The East German drums also appeared in some mail order catalogs. Most of the various combinations were identified numerically, but there were exceptions such as the "Supersonic".

From this time on, designs were once again strongly oriented on Sonor products. The state-qualified engineer Horst Eisermann managed the company from 1980 until its divestiture in 1990. After the fall of the Berlin Wall, attempts were made to sell the totally out-of-date facilities.

Tacton »Modell I« catalogued 1970s, bd 22", sn 14", tt 13", ft 16"

Tacton »Modell II« catalogued 1970s, bd 22", sn 14", tt 13", ft 16"

GDR 1945 - 1990

A wholesaler from Bavaria bought all of the remaining stock, which included metal cabinets full of drawings and documents. Among these were drawings of products and machines from manufacturers in the West that often were marked with the note "not realizable due to lack of material".

Today, many music shops still have large stocks of the metrical Tacton heads and/or the pedals with non-adjustable beaters.

By this point in the present chapter, some of you may be wondering why the Dresdner Apparatebau and its subsequent companies haven't been mentioned. It's a good point. This book, though, deals with drum sets, and the story of the Dresdner Apparatebau would take up a book of its own. That's why I will not even attempt to tell it here.

ROHEMA (RObert HEllinger MArkneukirchen)

The business Robert Hellinger founded in 1888 in Mark-neukirchen is known for its small percussion instruments and above all, for its sticks and mallets. After the Berlin Wall fell, the company once again began playing a role in the western part of Germany. Today, Mattias and Andreas Hellinger are the 5th generation managing the family business.

Altenburger Pergament & Trommelfell GmbH

In 1882, August Conrad founded the still-existing Altenburger Pergament & Trommelfell (drumhead) factory. Altenburg was a garrison city and also home to the drum manufacturer Wunderlich. These two factors meant there was a large need for drumheads there. At the beginning of the 1960s, the use of synthetic drumheads was on the rise and Altenburger manufactured them using a method similar to Karl Rimmel's. The world-wide high demand for synthetic heads meant Altenburger also supplied them to the (former) USSR, Cuba, China, Korea, Vietnam and other socialist countries. Rudolf Conrad, the founder's grandson, kept running the business until 1975. Then he too was forced to leave the company that had been in his family for 93 years and make way for the socialist planned economy. When the Wall fell in 1989, the company was put under the management of a trust. It was purchased from the trust by the Kotzenburg family in 1993. Replacement parts are still available here, especially for drums not made using international measurement norms.

Tacton »Modell III« catalogued 1970s
bd 22", sn 14", tt 13", ft 14", ft 16"

Tacton »Modell IV« catalogued 1970s
bd 22", sn 14", tt 12", tt 13", ft 16"

107

The History of Drums Made In Germany

Sources

Jacob, Friedrich. "Schlagzeug". 1991, ISBN 978-3-79-572343-9.
Ludwig, William F., Cook, Rob."The Making of a Drum Company". 2001, ISBN 1-888408-05-7.
Nicholls, Geof. "The Drum Book". 2008. ISBN 978-0-87930-940-4.
Paiste Profiles I – III. The Paiste Drummer Service. www. paiste.com.
Winterberg, Ingo. "Trix on Trixon – The Story of the German Drum Company". 2007, ISBN 978-3-00-026846-5.

Periodicals

Allgäuer Zeitung. March 3, 1983 and February 6, 1985
Jazz-Podium 1950s and 1960s
Musiker Fachblatt from 1975 – 1985

Interviews

Bong, Kurt; Campbell, Ruth; Hiseman, Jon; Karras, Sperri: Ludwig, William F. III; Lütz, Kerstin; Reichenbach, Hans-Jörg; Schneider, Martin; Steinmetz, Herbert; Thesing, Erich; Wieland, Harald; Winterberg, Ingo.

Framus: Helmut Hahn
Korri: Ute Göhlert, Herbert Fochler
Lefima: Käthe Fischer, Petra Ähnelt, Stefan Ähnelt
Luxor: Dieter Bay, Monika Hack, Josef Junginger
Offelder: Dirk Offelder, Peter Offelder
Rimmel: Leonhardt Rimmel, Hans Sattler, Reinhard Wranizka, Josef Jochum, Hans Meinelschmidt (†), Maria Reichel, Roswitha Ellis, Manfred Ambrosch, Peter Schätzl
Sonor: Horst Link (†), Karl Heinz Menzel, Peter Döpp, Martin Knebel
Tomsa: Hans Sattler (†), Karl Kailbert (†)
Trowa: Horst Eisermann, Gerd Veigl (†)

Others

Deutsches Patent- und Markenamt, München
Internet Sources used appear separately in the "Further information section".

Photos with kind permission of: Sonor GmbH, Ingo Winterberg, Musikhaus Rimmel, Hans Sattler, Familie Fischer-Ähnelt, Familie Offelder, Familie Sattler, Giannini Swiss Drums, Warwick GmbH & Co., Trowa.

The History of Drums Made In Germany

Index of Names

Adler Johannes 8,9,11
Aehnelt, Karl-Heinz 85
Aehnelt, Petra 85
Aehnelt, Stefan 85
Altenburger Pergament
& Trommelfell Gmbh 107
Althoff, Stefan 26
Ambrosch, Franz 43, 53
Ambrosch, Klaus 53
Ambrosch, Manfred 53, 109

Bamboos of Jamaika 50
Bay, Dieter, 109
Bickert, Manfred 52, 53
Binson 31
Blackfield 49
Bong, Kurt, 109

Campbell, Big Owen Fletchit 32, 50
Campbell, Ruth 109
Chuang, Arthur 27
Clarke, Kenny 18, 32
Concorde 78
Conrad, Rudolf 107

Dami 45
Deibel, Max 42, 43, 48, 76
Deri 16, 41ff, 48, 90
Deutsche Zelluloid Werke 38
Dixieland 100
Döpp, Peter 109
Dresdner Trommel- und
Apparatebau 10, 107
Drum Mate 20
Dunger 9, 11
DW 11

Echolette 91
Eisenak, U. 52f
Eisermann, Horst 106, 109
Ellington, Duke 32

Ellis, Roswitha 109
Evans, Chick 48

Fischer, Curt 82
Fischer, Ernst Albin 82
Fischer, Ernst Leberecht 82
Fischer, Käthe 82
Fleischer, Fips 84
Fochler, Herbert 109
Framus 97

Ganley, Alan 32
Giannini, Eugen 71,90, 97
Gibraltar 11
Glaser, Joe 17
Göhlert, Ute 109
GPL - Gustav Pouchard 10
Gretsch 5, 11, 20, 50
Gretsch, Friedrich 8
Grimsel, Martin 34
Grusche, Rudi 43

Hack 96, 99, 97
Hack, Monika 109
Hagström 31
Hahn, Helmut 53, 109
Hampton, Lionel 30, 32, 38
Heimrath, H. 52
Hellinger, Andreas 107
Hellinger, Matthias 107
Hellinger, Robert 107
Henkels, Kurt 85
Hess 11
Hiseman, Jon 109
Hohmann 90
Hohner 25, 26, 42
Hoshino Gakki 98
Hoshino Kouryou 96

Ibanez 98

Jakob, Friedrich 109
Jamaika Papa Curvin 50
Jochum, Josef 109
Josef, Junginger 109
JS Drums 97
Jürgens, Udo 50

Kailbert, Karl 79, 109
Kamm, Georg 43
Karras, Sperri, 109
Keck, Thomas 85
Kerbs, Marianne 107
Kiesant, Günter 85
Kings 78, 99
Knebel Martin 109
Korri (Korn & Riedel) 42, 78, 97, 106
Kotzenburg 107
Kronberger, Heinz 3
Kruse 11

Latin Percussion 11
Leedy 34
Lefima 10, 66, 81ff, 96, 105
Lindberg 98
Lineck 78, 99
Link, Andreas 19
Link, Angelika 19
Link, Helga 19
Link, Horst 18f, 23f, 25f, 109
Link, Johannes 14, 19
Link, Jörg 19
Link, Oliver 23
Link, Otto 15, 16, 28f, 104
Ludwig 4, 18, 20, 32, 104
Ludwig, Theobald 8
Ludwig, William 8
Ludwig, William F. III, 109
Lutter, Adalbert 85
Lutz, Kerstin, 109
Luxor 78, 96, 98

McEvans 49
Meinel & Herold 10,11,58
Meinelschmidt, Hans 43f, 109
Meinl 110f
Meinl, Roland 20, 98
Menzel, Karl-Heinz 23,24,26,109
Möhle, Siegfried 85
Mollenhauer 99
Müller & Bock 99
Music City 31, 33

Nazareth 53
Neckermann Versandhaus 100
Nicholls, Geoff 109

Oeschger, Artur 34
Offelder 89ff
Offelder, Dirk 92, 109
Offelder, Ernst 90
Offelder, Gitta 91f
Offelder, Joseph 92
Offelder, Peter 91f, 109
Offelder, Ursula 91

Paesold, Adolf 9
Paiste 11,13, 31
Papen, Frans 78
Paris, Teddy 17, 97
Pearl 20, 98
Pelzner, Walter 10
Pouchard, Gustav 10
Pückert 99
Purdie, Bernhard 26

Quelle Versandhaus 100

Reichel, Mari 109
Reichenbach, Hans-Jörg 109
Reisser 98
Remo 11, 36, 40, 50
Rich, Buddy 32

Rimmel 4, 47ff, 76, 78, 88, 90, 96
Rimmel, Karl 42, 52ff, 66f, 76, 107
Rimmel, Leonhardt 109
Rippen 33
Rizos, Awerinus 100
RKB 48, 76,100
Rogers 20, 34
Rohema 107
Röner, Erich 84
Roxy 78, 99, 101
Rudd, Phil 24

Sabian 25
Sandner, Franz 78
Sanner, Karl 17
Sattler & Co. OHG 76
Sattler, Franz 85ff, 78f, 109
Sattler, Hans 53ff
Schätzel, Peter 54ff, 125
Scherzer 11
Schimmel, Max 100
Schmidt, Bobby 17
Schmidtgen 76
Schneider, Martin, 109
Schuster & Co. 11
Seaman, Phil 32
Sehring, Rudi 17
Sindelfinger Holzringen 49
Slingerland 20, 30, 34
Smith, Steve 24
Sonor 15f, 34, 49, 51f, 53,59f, 82, 104,106
Spenke & Metzl 10
Spree City Stompers 85
St-Drums
St. Louis Music Supply Co. 33
Star 20, 98
Starr, Ringo 19, 32
Stockhausen, Karlheinz 45
Steinmetz, Herbert, 109
Strasmann, Ursula 92
Sweet, Darryl 53

Tacton 103ff, 72
Tama 98
Thesing, Erich, 109
Thissen 92
Thomas Organ Co. 33
Toca 11
Trixon 18,29ff,42,53,63ff,78,91,96,105
Tromsa 16, 75ff, 91, 96f
Trowa 16, 73,103ff
Troyan 97, 100
Tyrko 20

Veigl, Gerd 109
VOX 33, 35

Waldhauser, O. 52
Walter, Georg GeWa 11
Weimer, Karl Heinz 30ff
Westharzer Musikhaus 51
Wieland Harald, 109
Wilfer, Fred 97
Winterberg, Ingo 3, 34, 109
Wolfertz, Klaus 51
Wranizka, Reinhard 43, 109
Wunderlich 11

Zachow, Alex 100
Zen-On 20
Zeschky Gruppe 51
Zildjian 18, 25
Zildjian, Bob 25, 30f

The History of Drums Made In Germany

All internet links listed here are provided as a service and the following applies.
We have absolutely no influence on the design and content of the named links and herewith explicitly disclaim liability for all contents on these websites, nor do we endorse or claim ownership of the content. We can also provide no guarantee that the links are accessible at all times. They provided a helpful source of information while doing research for this book.

Altenburger Pergament & Trommelfell GmbH, Mozartstraße 8 , DE-04600 Altenburg
www.pergament-trommelfell.de

"Framus – built in the heart of Bavaria", Dr. Christian Hoyer 2007, ISBN 978-3-940448-00-2
www.framus-vintage.de

Leberecht Fischer KG, Barbaraweg 3, DE-93413 Cham
www.lefima.de

Music Professional Offelder GmbH, Roermonder Straße 370, DE- 52072 Aachen

Musikhaus Rimmel GmbH, Poststraße 7 - 9, DE-87435 Kempten,
www.musik-rimmel.de

Rohema Percussion OHG, Untere Tropitzschen 2, 08258 Markneukirchen,
www.rohema.de

Sonor GmbH, Zum Heilbach 5, DE-57319 Bad Berleburg www.sonor.com

The Original Sonor Museum (USA): www.sonormuseum.com

The Unofficial Virtual Museum: www.sonormuseum.de

The Hemelsoet Collection: www.vintagesonor.com

Sonor Signature Collection, Uwe Okunick www.sonor-signature.de

Sonor in Weissenfels, Klaus Rupple, ISBN-Nr. 978-3-936341-30-0
www.sonor-vintage-weissenfels.net

Folien, Kessel, metrische Felle, Vintage Parts
Schlagzeugrestauration Stegner, Emil –Kömmerling-Straße 1, DE-66954 Pirmasens
www.stdrums.de

Trixon
"Trix on Trixon – The Story of the German Drum Company", Ingo Winterberg 2007, ISBN 978-3-00-026846-5,
"The Trixon Collection", Ingo Winterberg 2010, ISBN 978-3-00-030689-1,
verlag@trixondrums.de
Service:
Ingo Winterberg, Tel.: +49 (0) 5404-6403, info@trixondrums.de,
www.trixondrums.de

TROWA, Rudolf-Haym-Straße 33, DE- 06110 Halle/ Saale,
www.trowamusic.com

www.ingramcontent.com/pod-product-compliance
Lightning Source LLC
Chambersburg PA
CBHW081726100526
44591CB00016B/2513